The Way to Trade
Better

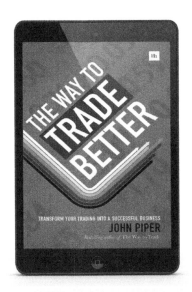

The Way to Trade *Better*

Transform your trading into a successful business

John Piper

HARRIMAN HOUSE LTD
18 College Street
Petersfield
Hampshire
GU31 4AD
GREAT BRITAIN
Tel: +44 (0)1730 233870
Email: enquiries@harriman-house.com
Website: www.harriman-house.com

First published in Great Britain in 2016
Copyright © John Piper

Print ISBN: 978-0-85719-336-0
eBook ISBN: 978-0-85719-532-6

British Library Cataloguing in Publication Data
A CIP catalogue record for this book can be obtained from the British Library.

ABOUT THE AUTHOR

John Piper has been trading markets since the mid-1980s, mainly writing options but also trading futures, spread betting and binary betting. The highlights have been trading right through the '87 crash (mainly selling put options – hence the lack of hair!), annual turnover exceeding £2m of option premiums on his personal account, winning a TV trading contest, and generally spending far too much time glued to screens.

Whilst abusing himself in this way he also decided to help other traders and started *The Technical Trader* in 1989 which has become the leading trading newsletter in the UK. The newsletter filled a void and the business has helped many traders over the years.

John has also developed a number of trading techniques; he summarises his approach as *psycho-trading* – meaning getting into the mind of the market.

John spends time in the Spanish hills around Marbella but is also a frequent traveller to more exotic climes, often with the Hash House Harriers – a club for those who like a drink but who have a running problem!

John runs a trading service looking for the *big* calls. He enjoys working with other traders to help develop their skills and will also provide funds and/or business ideas as appropriate.

Also by John Piper

- *The Way to Trade*
- *The Fortune Strategy*
- *Profit Before Work*
- *Binary Betting*
- *Binary Trading*
- *Tunnel Trading*
- *The Business of Trading*
- *The KrautGap/ZeitGap Modules/The A-B Trading System* (awarded 'Best Financial Product 2014' by *More Money Review*)
- *Trading Triangles*
- *Wealth is a Choice*

If you would like to receive John's free news sheet enter your details on this page: **www.johnpiper.info/jptt.htm** (you will also receive a free copy of *Wealth is a Choice*).

The author welcomes feedback and can be contacted at **john@ bigcall.co.uk**; his website is **www.johnpiper.info**.

ACKNOWLEDGEMENTS

I owe a big debt of gratitude to both Les Meehan, Success Coach Extraordinaire, who has carefully read the manuscript and made many useful and excellent additions, including writing a chapter in the appendices, and my publisher, Stephen Eckett, who has, as usual, gone well beyond the call of duty.

FOREWORD BY TONY PLUMMER

Whether one trades for oneself or on behalf of others, success is defined not just in terms of accumulated wealth. It is also defined in terms of emotional independence from the ups and downs of financial markets. A competent trader should be able to take the rough with the smooth and remain confident that – eventually – he or she will still come out ahead. The problem, however, is that the journey from early aspiration to actual achievement is a long one. It takes time, commitment, and experience. Indeed, as John Piper points out in this potentially life-changing book, the journey is ultimately one of personal transformation. A successful career in financial market trading will inevitably alter both the way that you deal with yourself and the way you deal with others.

A journey that involves personal transformation will present profound challenges. The benefits are immense, but so are the hurdles that have to be overcome; and there are a number of such hurdles. First, a trading position involves not just the ownership of a trading position but also an emotional commitment to the performance of that position. In a very important sense, therefore, a trading position can become a part of one's sense of self. A trade that goes wrong can be felt directly as an existential threat; a trade that goes right can be interpreted as evidence of infallibility. One important objective for a successful trader, therefore, will be to ensure that one's emotional life is not buffeted by the rise and fall of asset prices.

The second hurdle facing a trader is the emotional contagion that constellates around a specific bullish or bearish narrative in a market. It is not sufficiently widely recognised that human beings are programmed to take notice of others' behaviour. In part this is to ensure co-operation; but, in part too, it is to ensure that unexpected information – which, in Gregory Bateson's words are those "differences that make a difference" – can quickly be transmitted to others. If we feel sure that any currently arising threat will immediately be made known to us by others, we can carry on doing what we want to do. In my opinion, it is this particular survival mechanism that is the basis of collective behaviour and hence of predictable patterns and trends in asset prices. One potential objective for a successful trader, therefore, is to become familiar with the forces that drive a market, while remaining aloof from the emotional contagion that forms them.

This, in turn, implies two further hurdles: the creation of a practical methodology for taking advantage of price patterns and trends, and the honing of an ability to make decisions that utilise that methodology and that are not overridden by other people's opinions. Both of these relate to our ability to make decisions that are correct for us.

The third hurdle, therefore, is the finding and implementation of a trading system that handles the ebb and flow of market prices. As John Piper points out, this is a personal endeavour. There is no right or wrong way of trading; all that really matters is whether the end result is a financial profit. Establishing viable entry and exit signals is therefore an important task in its own right. It will take research and – ultimately – experience to achieve the desired results. It is not something that can be achieved overnight. A successful trader will therefore have invested a great deal of time in formulating trading strategies and in testing them out. He or she will also – and as a result – have great confidence in those strategies.

The fourth hurdle is to be able to make decisions correctly. In my opinion, too few people fully understand the deep involvement of their own physical chemistry in the decision-making process. It is important to understand that each of us can actually know from the messages generated by our feelings whether or not a decision is right for us. This could be very relevant in constructing a robust trading system. It is also likely to be relevant when adjustments subsequently need to be made to that system.

And then, of course, there is the problem of dealing with pressure from others. I remember the great protagonist of the Elliott Wave Principle, Robert Prechter, observing many years ago that some of the best financial market traders are those with a military background. The reason that Robert offered was that such individuals would ignore others' opinions and stick to their trading rules. Unfortunately, relatively few of us are born with this particular ability. In fact, quite the reverse is true because cultural convention argues that the human brain makes decisions. What is missed is the fact that the brain can only process data; so it can only reach decisions when it is able to access prior assumptions based on cultural mores, market imperatives, and peer group pressures. Such decisions may be appropriate within the context of wider groupings, but they may not be directly appropriate for the person making them. Ultimately, therefore, a successful trader will be able to formulate and maintain a workable decision-making process by using the information generated by the wider concept of 'mind'. This involves an awareness of personal feelings and their relevance.

Under these circumstances, it is not surprising that the successful trader is a significantly different person to the one that originally thought it might be a good idea to become involved with financial markets. However, as in all great endeavours, that journey is made significantly easier if guidance is at hand. This is why John Piper's book is so valuable. It comprehensively covers the territory of objective trading within a highly subjective environment, and it is easy to understand. It covers not just the psychology of trading but also important practical matters such as Money Management. Some of his own experiences, which are outlined in the book, reveal his personal journey through the trading landscape, and many of us will easily recognise the truth of his testimony. The fact that he, himself, has had a long and successful career trading confirms that he has faced the issues directly and dealt with them appropriately. It is to all our benefit that he is offering some of his wisdom to a wider audience.

Tony Plummer
January 2016

PREFACE

If you are an individual trader, whether a novice or experienced, you will benefit from reading this book because:

1. It *is* possible to make money in the markets consistently. It *is* possible to beat the market. The author, among many others, has done it. To do the same you need to follow a proven methodology which suits your personality. This book explains this process and how to build on it to make trading your business.

2. This book sets out a number of proven methodologies, giving you a head start in selecting one which will work for you.

3. This book follows on from *The Way to Trade* and takes a number of *big* steps forward. John Piper wrote *The Way to Trade* in 1998 because he had never come across a book which dealt with the whole issue of trading. There are many books which deal with market analysis and technical analysis techniques. There are many books which deal with psychology. There are books which deal with Money Management and all manner of other subjects; some even cover a range of topics. But no other book covered it all, from a successful philosophy of trading, through all the psychology, to the methodologies, the operation thereof, and the end result.

4. It is rare to find a book which appreciates that it is no good doing it "how I say". We each have to find our own route to success.

5. Trading financial markets offers huge potential for gain. Perhaps more importantly, you can make money whether markets go up or down.

Interested?

Anyone who is into trading and wants to be more successful will get value out of this book.

Why this book is unique

Trading is a life experience; it is not like any other business. As you become a better trader, you can become a better, more effective, person – often by overcoming internal psychological challenges encountered on the trading journey. But as you evolve it is difficult to look back at where you were. Those traders who do make it often forget how they got there; not surprisingly, as a lot of the skills become subconscious. They become winning habits!

However, I have always combined trading with writing about markets. This has given me a fairly unique insight and forced me to express personal matters which other traders just assume. It has also forced me to more carefully examine the precise process involved in becoming a successful trader. It is solely through this process that I discovered the Trading Pyramid. This was the first attempt to create a model for trading success and traders will find it immensely useful. (This was covered in *The Way to Trade*.)

So not only does this book take the trader right through from the beginning to the end result (trading profits, lots of them!) it also provides a framework, both practical and psychological, with which to work.

There are no right or wrong ways to trade

The only thing that counts is the result. This book sets out a range of parameters within which to build the system that suits you. The beauty of trading is that it becomes an expression of your own personality. Good traders don't do, they simply are. To become a good trader you have got to find the approach which will work for you. This book will help you do just that.

Follow your own path

To get there you must follow your own path. It is no good following the trades other people make. Certainly you need help to learn this business, which is what this book is all about. You will need a mentor, but you do not need gurus who tell you how to trade. You will only win by trading your way. Indeed Frank Sinatra's big hit *My Way* is an excellent anthem for any trader. Taking that step to do it by yourself is one many traders find the most difficult, but it is essential.

How this book is structured

In the Introduction I establish the major concept that trading is a business. If you want a profitable business allowing you total financial freedom you need to have regard to the five key pillars of that business.

These five pillars are:

1. Focus

2. Style

3. Right Trading

4. Right Size

5. Successful Habits

Added together these assist in the Transformation necessary to take you to where you are reaping the rewards from running this business. That essentially is the purpose of this book.

I say "assist" because each individual has to provide their own drive and determination. Not only that, but we each bear a unique relationship with the concept of money and serious work may be required to develop that relationship so you can trade successfully. Do not mistake this process with any idea of getting rich quick!

In **Section 1**, I expand upon these concepts and explain how each of the pillars interact and form key parts of your business.

In **Section 2**, I introduce a further key concept – your Trading System. You need to apply the five pillars to this concept to create the winning habits which provide the Transformation.

In **Section 3**, I introduce the important topic of Money Management.

In **Section 4**, I look at 'Your Psychology Techniques' which will become the foundation stone of your success.

In **Section 5**, I examine 'Good Habits and Bad Habits' – this is a key section for those who have traded previously and have built up a range of bad habits. In this section I carefully explain the bad habits many traders have formed and suggest ways to transform these into successful habits.

In **Section 6**, I provide 'A Step-by-Step Guide to Trading Professionally' – this can be considered the most important part of the book. It gives you a timetable, in three-monthly segments, to help achieve your goals.

CONTENTS

INTRODUCTION

LET ME TELL YOU A STORY ...

Once upon a time there was a trader and in 1985 he put on his first trade and it lost money.

The same thing happened with his next trade. On the third occasion the market moved as he expected but, as he was new to this, he grabbed the small profit he had and squandered the big profit that lay just around the corner.

After these three trades, in 1985-86 (his trading frequency was very low at this time) he was lying in a hot bath after a hard day's skiing in Andorra and pondered a new trading approach a friend had suggested to him.

He was sure it would be a winner!

In April 1987 he started to trade the new approach and, after some fairly frantic trading, he was up £500 after a couple of weeks. Not bad back then!

He had just quit a very high-paying job and had a manor house and a 911 Turbo to support, not to mention his wife and daughter. He thought he'd found the solution.

He went at it with gusto. And promptly lost £4000 the next month.

The next few months were generally positive. He also sold the manor house, so his coffers were overflowing with cash.

In July 1987 the market peaked and the analysis technique he used called for the fall to continue. He built up a large short position

1

(£500 per point!). But in the middle of October 1987 he reduced the position by 60% based on a short-term pattern and thus failed to fully capitalise on the very large move that followed.

On the morning of Monday 18 October 1987 he sold all remaining positions for a £20,000 profit – very far from shabby back then!

But at the same time he continued to operate his system as the 1987 crash continued and he became very exposed to the downside.

Only by great good fortune did he avoid being wiped out during the next few months as the market went broadly sideways. This allowed him to get out at break-even.

The family moved to the fishing village of Lerici in Italy and he continued to trade the system, racking up a £20,000 gain in one month. Life was good!

In 1989, during a trip to Israel, the market experienced another big move and this time he was not so lucky – he was wiped out!

That trader was, of course, me. This book is partly about how *not* to do what I did then. More importantly, it's about how to make your trading the true source of success and financial freedom it can be.

When I wrote *The Way to Trade* back in the 1990s I subtitled it 'Discover your successful trading personality', but it is now clear that, for many of us, discovering it is one thing and making it into a successful business is something entirely different.

This new book is all about making your trading into a successful business and I have created a five-step process for this:

1. Getting your **focus** right – your focus determines your trading arena.

2. Getting your **style** right – finding your way to make money in this area of the markets.

3. Getting the **trading** right – i.e. maximising the points on your trades.

4. Increasing **size** – making the money: this is where it starts to pay!

5. Making all this a **winning habit** – this is when it pays year after year after year.

Each step will pose challenges and at each level it is critical to identify any issues you may have which are preventing you from completing each stage. These issues may be technical, emotional or behavioural. Once identified, you then need to overcome these issues, and each will require a different approach.

This is all about *Transformation* – transforming you from where you are now to where you want to be! Transformation means permanent change, not temporary fixes.

A big part of this is that final stage, making these new *habits* that together form your new trading persona.

Much of the material in this book has come from direct client contact (for example, I refer you to an interesting trade by one of my clients that can be found in Appendix 4).

To conclude this introduction let me spell out the function of this book and who it is aimed at:

- If you want to **make your trading into a successful business** you are in precisely the right place. I will show you the key steps you need to take.

- If you are **just starting out as a trader** but your goal is the same then again you are in precisely the right place. I have written this book, and its predecessor, so they are accessible to those with and without experience.

Maybe you are not that serious, maybe you just want to make money – or make more money – in the markets. Again, you will find the techniques discussed in these pages are exactly what you are looking for.

My aim is to show you the way – to trade better!

John Piper
January 2016

PS The vast majority of material in this book has been specifically written for inclusion herein. The exceptions are details of the trading systems I have included in Appendices 1 and 2 which have previously been made available to those who either bought that particular system or who subscribed to my Big Call service.

PPS This is the second book in *The Way to Trade* series and it is not the last, God willing! I have already put pen to paper on book three – *The Way to Trade Robotically* – which is about using trading robots to run your trading business.

Section 1 – The Five Pillars of Success

I SAID IN THE INTRODUCTION THAT MAKING YOUR TRADING INTO A successful business is a five-step process. You may also call these the five pillars of your business. Here they are:

1. Focus

2. Right style

3. Right trading

4. Right size

5. Making these winning habits (aka transformation)

Let's now look at these five pillars in more detail.

1. FOCUS

Focus is one of the strongest weapons in your arsenal as a trader.

It determines how you look at the market. More importantly it determines what you ignore. Given the massive amount of information any market produces, you need to ignore most of it.

For some, focus may mean reading the *Financial Times* or the *Wall Street Journal*; for others it may mean weekly meetings with brokers or advisers; for others it may mean looking at charts; or maybe you have bought a short-term trading system and your focus is on its rules.

You will understand immediately that each of these different viewpoints will give a very different picture. The person who reads what a commentator has written in the *Wall Street Journal* will have a very different perspective from someone who is following a short-term trading system. Here are a few of the areas which will vary:

- **Time frame** – this can vary from a few minutes to a few months or years.

- **Market** – there are stock markets, futures markets, commodity markets, not to mention spread betting and binary betting markets, and each offers the trader a variety of risk and opportunity.

- **Objective** – some want long-term gains and dividends, others want short-term trading profits, with a vast array between those two extremes.

But even if you get a match on those three there is still enormous variance in how any one trader may decide to **extract profit** from the market. For example, one of my trading colleagues looks to profit from market gaps whereas I prefer trading spikes; others use Japanese candlesticks or moving averages … the list is virtually endless.

Focus determines exactly what you look at. Later in this book I give an outline of a trading system I use called *ZeitGap* which is based on the German DAX index. To trade this system your focus will be entirely on the following factors:

1. The prior close on the DAX.

2. The early action as the DAX opens.

And that's it!

I am using *ZeitGap* merely to help illustrate a number of important points. At the same time I am happy to give you the basic idea behind this system which I use daily to extract cash from the markets.

You also need to have regard to Money Management, but the trading system takes care of risk control. So your focus is *very* restricted and thus the whole business of trading becomes *much* simpler.

Compare these two factors with those a value investor may wish to consider before buying any shares:

1. Company accounts (plus expert help to decipher them)

2. Overall economic situation

3. Earnings trends

4. True asset value

5. Breakdown value

I could continue to add to this list fairly indefinitely but I think I have made the point. The more you define your focus, the less you have to worry about. Becoming an expert in a very limited range of items is much easier than becoming an expert in a much larger range of areas.

To take *ZeitGap* as an example, it takes very little time to become an expert in the basic rules and the operation of the system. There are then a number of additional, more advanced techniques you can add as you progress. Each of these techniques adds to the bottom line and each technique takes its own time to learn – none very complex. A professional trader will tend to extend this process and continually evolve, testing out new techniques as they go forward.

To conclude this point: I have been active in markets for over 26 years and I have met and worked with many professional traders; in every case they have a clear focus and they have made it their business to become expert in that focus!

2. RIGHT STYLE

The first edition of *The Way to Trade* was subtitled 'Discover Your Successful Trading Personality'. This trading personality is essentially your 'style'.

There are many, many different ways to trade and even when you have decided on your focus there are a large variety of ways in which to trade that focus.

For example, your focus may throw out daily market targets (you may call these 'magnets') and your focus may be to trade from the open towards that target. But some traders may adopt a relaxed style, simply placing a limit at, or near, the target and an appropriate stop before they leave for the golf course.

Another trader may adopt a far more aggressive style. Perhaps carefully watching the opening action and quickly closing if it does not go the right way, or moving stops quickly to lock in profit if the market does go the right way.

In both cases there is the same, or very similar, focus but very different styles.

Which style is better?

That may depend on how much you like golf! But more importantly it will depend on whether the trader is getting what he wants. If both traders are expert in their approach then their styles may well be equally good and give them what they want (but these may be different things, of course).

Your style of trading will also depend on your personality and psychology. You could say your trading style is a reflection of your personality, your core values, and your beliefs.

3. RIGHT TRADING

The concept of 'right trading' is straightforward but involves two distinct strands:

1. Your **focus must give you an edge** – an expectancy of profit over time.

2. You must **trade it correctly** so you realise this edge.

The first goes to the essence of a professional trader and means carefully testing out your focus to ensure it is a money-making proposition. You are responsible for how you trade and you need to test carefully to ensure your approach will make you money.

The second phase is simply trading well to realise the positive expectancy of your approach. Once you are doing so and are confident that you will continue to do so you are ready to move on to …

4. RIGHT SIZE

This is when you start to be in business for real.

The key points are important:

1. You have defined your **focus**.

2. You have become expert in these areas and developed your **style**.

3. You have carefully tested out the components of your trading in the markets and know that you have an **edge**.

4. You have **proven this in real-time trading**.

5. You understand the key concepts of **Money Management** (part of your style).

Once these factors are in place you *must* increase the size of your trades if you wish to make serious money as a trader. As you progress, and if you have got it right, your account size will grow and you can continue to increase the size of your trades.

You need to have regard to *Money Management*. At its simplest this means not risking too much on any one trade.

My suggestion is that you should set your risk parameters at between 2% and 4% per trade. That means that you take your total trading pot (say £10,000) and risk between £200 to £400 per trade – as a rule of thumb it is better to risk less rather than more.

This may seem low but you need to realise that losses will happen and you have to be able to deal with these without serious depletion of capital. For example, if your trading approach gives you 50% winners and 50% losers (this is quite usual but your winners need to be bigger than your losers on average to give you that much-needed edge) then every 1000 trades you will, statistically, see a consecutive string of 11 or more losers.

No one expects this, unless they are familiar with statistics, but if you were trading at 10% risk per trade you could be wiped out.

Plus bear in mind that if you halve your account size you then have to double it (achieve a 100% profit) just to get back to where you started from. Such an achievement is not easy, so it's best not to halve your account size in the first place.

By risking 2% to 4% (and basing this on your pot as it increases and decreases), you minimise the effect of the inevitable losers and you are still around to make hay when you see a string of 11 winners (also statistically likely, but no one ever complains about that!).

Here, again, psychology will be involved in your risk management. If you are of the type who thrives on high-risk and excitement, take extra care not to allow these tendencies to lead you to ignore the above recommendations.

Money can raise many psychological issues but, the fact remains, you will need to deal with this stuff if you want to make trading your business. If you are emotionally a poor loser in competitive situations this may negatively impact on your ability to deal with the inevitable financial losses you will experience when trading.

As you work on this, you will automatically ...

5. MAKE THESE WINNING HABITS

Most of what we do as human beings are habits. Some of us adopt winning habits and become wealthy and successful. Most people, for whatever reason, adopt losing habits and struggle.

A lot of this may have to do with the human instinct to herd – you need only look in your local pub, or at a football stadium or rock concert, to see how we love to herd together.

The people who succeed tend to be those who are happy to go it alone and to do things differently. They are also people who have a very positive *success attitude*; they view success, wealth, and successful people as desirable and inspiring.

Later in this book we will be looking at how the herd generally approach trading and why they lose. If you want to win you must *not* do these things and you *do* need to adopt the processes set out in this section. These processes are at root fairly simple. If you keep doing them they become resourceful, successful habits (as opposed to the destructive habits which are all too common among the majority of traders).

We are all too prone to adopt bad habits and these need to be eliminated. This can be a lot easier to say than to do. As an example I decided I was drinking too much alcohol and in November 2012 I cut out alcohol for a full year.

I found this easy to do and I think I had managed to self-hypnotise myself. In any case it was no great problem having zero alcohol for the year. I was concerned that if I started to drink again in November 2013 that I would be right back where I started. I was pleasantly surprised to find, instead, that I was able to take or leave alcohol pretty much at will.

I am not saying that bad habits may not return but, for now, I have eliminated the old and am much happier with the new.

Remember, a habit is formed by repeating an activity and your subconscious mind doesn't know or care if the habit produced is good or bad.

In terms of your trading, you need to identify and isolate the bad habits you have built up and then eliminate them. Again, this is much easier said than done – bear in mind many of our habits keep us alive on a daily basis, so most of them are extremely useful!

Unfortunately, too often many of our habits subtly undermine our attempts at success. When we start to look at peak performance in any area we need to change our less useful habits to succeed – we will be looking at this in greater detail in Section Five.

Finally, I will add what I might term a sixth pillar: the ability to *take control*. You cannot be a successful professional trader unless you decide what you want and you go out to get it. *The Way to Trade* was all about developing *your* successful trading personality and that is part of it. Decide what you want and go out and get it!

It goes beyond this too, as you need to actively increase stake size and learn to deal with that at each stage. Your unique relationship with money may be a key factor in this process.

This five or six-step process outlined above works well in all aspects of life, suitably modified as required.

Let's now look briefly at the **Trading Pyramid**.

THE TRADING PYRAMID

Above I introduced you to the five pillars of your trading business. To recap:

1. Focus

2. Right style

3. Right trading

4. Right size

5. Making these winning habits

Within these five pillars you also need to get to grips with the **Trading Pyramid**. The diagram below shows the pyramid.

I explain the Trading Pyramid fully in *The Way to Trade* and I do not want to repeat that material. However, it is worth giving a basic introduction here as this will be useful for all readers.

The various levels of the pyramid can be grouped under the following three headings:

1. Trading System

2. Money Management

3. Your Psychology

1. Trading System

This is your *system* for extracting cash from the markets. Believe me, the markets are very willing to give you money as long as you approach them in the right way – meaning if you use what I am teaching you.

You need to be aware that if you approach the markets in the *wrong* way they can be voracious in taking your hard-earned cash away from you – so be warned!

Your Trading System includes the top five levels of the pyramid, albeit the very top level (Profits/Losses) is more the result of all prior levels rather than a part of any particular level.

2. Money Management

This grouping includes the levels Money Management and Risk Control.

3. Your Psychology

The third factor is *knowing yourself*, or to be more precise it is knowing the psychology with which you approach the markets. This includes the bottom three levels of the pyramid.

In particular it is all about ensuring your psychology remains cool, calm and collected as you place your trades – for you are in for one hell of a ride, that I can promise you.

You will be totally safe as long as you follow the rules – be sure not to forget that.

As we go forward I will explain how the five pillars tie in with the Trading Pyramid. Simply put, the five pillars are a process during which you acquire the skills to use the various levels of the pyramid.

The following three sections address these three groupings in turn. First up: Trading Systems.

Section 2 –
Trading Systems

INTRODUCING THE TRADING IDEA

IN THIS SECTION I AM GOING TO INTRODUCE WHAT I CALL THE *trading idea*. By this I mean the pattern of market action on which we base our trading system. We then build on the trading idea to construct that trading system.

What we are looking for (what every successful trader needs) is an *edge* – an advantage so that we make money.

Without an edge we will always be at a disadvantage.

What we are looking for are low-risk trading opportunities, where the *risk is strictly controlled* and the *potential profit is excellent.* So if we lose (and this is bound to happen in the markets from time to time) we only lose a little and when we win, we have the opportunity to win big. Excellent profits may be generated through size or through frequency, meaning we have a high hit rate.

Please read that paragraph again to make sure you have fully understood it.

So you can see how important it is to have a trading edge – it is the foundation stone of all that follows. We certainly do not want to trade randomly. Although we may place bets on which way a market will move, this is *not* gambling in the conventional sense.

The term 'gambling' needs some attention. There is an inference with this word that money is being tossed to the winds with a small hope some of it may return; and this may well apply to 90% of traders who lose 90% of their cash in 90 days. But it does *not* apply to you and you may call yourself a professional trader or a professional gambler – at the end of the day the two terms are interchangeable. It is the term *professional* which is essential!

In this sense professional means you treat your trading like a serious business.

I believe the trading idea has to incorporate the Three Simple Rules, which is one of the levels of the Trading Pyramid.

THE THREE SIMPLE RULES

For any trading idea to work it needs to pay attention to these three key trading rules:

1. Cut your losses

2. Run your profits

3. Trade selectively

Trading rule 1: Cut your losses

This rule simply means you never lose more than a small or acceptable sum. You get to choose exactly what is meant by these terms – you choose what is small and acceptable to you.

The mechanism for this seeming miracle when trading is something called a *stop*, whereby you exit a position at a predetermined point if the price goes against you. An alternative is to trade in smaller size so that a total loss (i.e. the instrument in question goes to zero) would still be acceptable; however most traders want the gearing. Gearing, of course, is a double-edged sword.

When buying options and trading binary options (aka binary bets) the total purchase sum is the total risk. When writing options matters become more complex (there is a large section on this in *The Way to Trade* and I do not plan to extend it here).

Trading rule 2: Run your profits

The first rule keeps you safe and ensures you live to fight another day after a losing trade (or even a series of them – it can and does happen). This second rule brings home the bacon.

Most traders don't lose through taking too many losses; they lose through not making hay when the sun shines. Most traders never give themselves a chance because they take profits *too early*.

Small losses *and* small profits = zilch!

You need to avoid this trap if you are to win and break into a world of abundance.

Psychologically you need both courage and fortitude. Don't allow fear, or any other negative emotion for that matter, to create a trap and then dictate your actions.

Running profits does not mean you must always leave positions open in the hope that the market will keep going the right way. It is perfectly OK to use profit targets, for example. A profit target merely means you take profits at a predefined point and this is something that many systems do automatically (as does *ZeitGap* – see Appendix 2).

Such a profit target can be fairly close. The idea is that you let the market reach that point, unless you have a valid reason for bailing out earlier.

Trading rule 3: Trade selectively

The third rule adds the icing to the cake. If you only take the best trades then you achieve a double whammy – you get better profits and you eliminate a portion of losses.

I have a number of ways of filtering out the trades I do not want whilst limiting losses when trades go against me – we will be looking at this later.

These three trading rules are fundamental to your success and we are going to apply them as we go through this section.

It is interesting that these three rules impact on your trading system but also form part of your Money Management system; they are therefore important to two of the three factors of the Trading Pyramid (your Trading System and Money Management). They then feed through to your psychology (the third factor) as they keep you relaxed and in control.

TWO TRADING SYSTEMS

At this point I am going to refer you to two trading systems I use in my everyday trading. These offer good examples of what I have explained in the book so far.

The two trading systems are:

1. *Xtreme Stop* (in full)

2. *ZeitGap* (in outline)

You can find both these systems explained in the Appendices. (By the way, just because they are in the Appendices it does not mean they can be skipped. The sections explaining these systems contain some of the most useful information in the whole book.)

The reason I am introducing these systems at this point is that I want to refer to these in the rest of the book.

Both systems are essentially very simple. In fact I have now developed a trading robot to trade *ZeitGap* for me. I mention this as it demonstrates the essence of the trading business, at least as far as I am concerned. Business is about maximising the cash flowing in whilst minimising the effort involved!

CUTTING LOSSES – USING STOPS

Above, in 'Trading rule 1: Cut your losses', I referred to using stops. I want to say some more about stops here.

First I must explain how stops work.

Stops are simplicity itself. The stop is placed at a specified level and if the price hits the stop level the trade is activated (usually to close a position). In other words, you will have your trade closed automatically if the price hits your predetermined stop. You don't have to be there watching the screen.

The mechanics vary depending on whether your initial trade is a buy or a sell, but they are merely the mirror image of each other. I give two examples in Appendix 2 using my *ZeitGap* system.

Using stops is a fairly important part of the trading process, so be sure you understand this before moving on.

Stops are useful but not miraculous

Before we continue, I need to tell you that while stops may seem miraculous when you first encounter them, they can seem like demons from hell after you use them for a while.

The fundamental issue is that very few aspects of trading markets are always one way. The systems I use have a great edge but *will not work all the time*. Stops will keep you safe but every now and then you will be stopped out of a good trade, meaning a trade that would have gone on to win if you had not used a stop.

This can be highly frustrating. You take your trade and place your stop, you look at the action, see the market has hit your profit target, and start to celebrate yet another win. Then you look a bit more closely and see that your account has shrunk not grown.

How can this be?

Then you see that, before going the right way, the market shot off in the wrong direction and stopped you out. This can become a major headache when trading markets.

There are two things which reduce the danger:

1. The **edge itself needs to be significant** so that most trades will win and the stops will not come into play very often, plus

2. We can use a fairly **wide stop**.

This second point needs some amplification.

I have a saying, "Fear creates what is feared." For example, my step-daughter has a fear of dogs and because this is so acute she is always looking around in case a dog is near. The result: she keeps seeing dogs and gets nervous, the dogs sense this and react. So her very fear creates what is feared.

Stops are the same.

You need a stop otherwise losses can become overbearing, but you need to be relaxed not fearful. The stop needs to be a fair way away, not so close that it does not allow the trade to breathe. Bear in mind that the market is an organic entity composed of all the people participating in it. It needs to breathe in and out, up and down. You don't want your stop to be triggered by this natural movement.

Many traders get this wrong and I believe it is one of the four foremost causes of failure in the markets, so do not make this mistake.

Choosing the stop level

Choosing the stop level is a trade-off between minimising the amount you lose when the stop is hit and minimising the number of times your stops are hit.

However, these two criteria are mutually exclusive in that the former requires a very close stop and the latter one that is further away. I'm sure you can see that if you set a stop just one point away from your opening level, it would be hit very frequently, but your loss each time would be small. Conversely, if you set the stop 500 points away it would rarely be hit, but when it did get hit you would lose a lot of money.

What a stop is *not* there for is to stop you out frequently, thereby preventing you from making any money. But believe it or not that is how most traders use stops: making them far too close to market action. Tight stops like that are an invitation for the market to profit at your expense.

It can be hugely frustrating to be taken out of a good trade by a stop which is too tight. It's *so* annoying to see yourself taken out, then the market happily goes off in exactly the direction you predicted as you watch the money you *would* have made, getting ever larger.

A further factor to bear in mind is that the stop you choose needs to relate to your style of trading. Very short-term traders can use very tight stops (allowing higher gearing and position size), but this option is not available if your trade is designed to catch longer-term moves. It is valid to enter a longer-term trade via a shorter-term mechanism, but you would need a more relaxed stop policy as the trade progresses.

You may think I am making a real meal of this, but this information is critically important. As I just said, most traders get this very wrong.

Now I want to say something more about running your profits (Trading rule 2).

RUN YOUR PROFITS

We have just looked at the first big mistake traders make, *placing stops too tightly*, and now we must look at the second, *taking profits too early*. For the record the other two are trading far too often and not trading in sufficient size.

All of these are driven by our enemies: fear and greed. In fact these tend to drive all the major mistakes. The exception being not putting in sufficient work, which stems from lack of commitment and laziness.

It is **fear of loss** which makes amateur traders place stops too tightly. They just can't bear to see those losses mounting up. They would rather cut and run than see the trade slip further into the red.

Similarly it is **pure greed** that makes people grab profits early. They need the hit of pleasure which comes from winning the trade. Only when they close the trade and take the money can they reassure themselves that they have won. Trouble is they've left most of the money on the table.

Let me give you a simple example – a sweet shop. Let's say the assistant makes a small mistake and rather than pricing the Fruit & Nut at 95p he prices it at 85p. The shop sells 200 bars of Fruit & Nut every week and thus loses £20 (10p × 200 = £20) which is about £1,000 every year and £10,000 every decade.

Sweet shops do not necessarily make a great deal of money with all the various overheads. A £10,000 hole is very hard to fill; in fact it may make the difference between success and closure if the business is a bit marginal to start with.

In the trading world the sums at stake are far bigger than 10p on a bar of Fruit & Nut! It is *very* easy to take a trading profit early and leave £100 or even £1,000 on the table. Those amounts add up over a few years and can make the difference between a comfortable lifestyle and bumping along.

Let's take a system which trades every other day as an example. Every trading month usually has around 20 trading days, so let's say we trade ten times per month and with each trade we leave £100 or £1000 on the table. 10 × £100 is £1,000 a month, and 10 × £1,000 is £10,000 a month!

You simply cannot afford to throw away that sort of money, especially as you have to cover the losses that inevitably will also come your way.

Here is what most traders do: they place the stops too close so they are losing out to the stop far too often *and* they take profits far too early, so they *never make the big money*. The result is they simply spin their wheels taking lots of small loses and small profits – they may even end up slightly in profit over a year but if so it may just about pay for a beaten-up VW, not for a new Porsche 911 Turbo!

What does it mean to run your profits?

It is a phrase open to different interpretations, but in the context of a system which uses profit targets it simply means **do not bail out with 20 points when you have a 60 point trade to exploit**. Okay, you might decide to add a rule that allows you to take 55 points rather than 60 after a certain time of day, and there can be good reason for that, but don't settle for 20.

In terms of **longer-term trading**, it is somewhat different as a trade can last for months and so the key skill is to stay with the trade as long as is possible, but at the same time being aware when the move may be over. This is a fairly fine line and is beyond what we can achieve in a book of this size.

What I can do is mention a few of the simpler techniques that may prove useful:

- Use a trailing stop which means you keep moving your stop to lock in ever more profit; one technique is to use key highs (when short) or key lows (when long) which the market makes as it moves in your direction and place stops a little beyond such highs or lows.

- Take some profit from time to time, but leave most of the position in place – this may be particularly useful if the market hits obvious levels where it may change direction.

- Take all profits if you see a clear signal to trade the other way (and maybe trade it).

- Don't get suckered into an early exit.

Be warned, it is one of the challenges of market action, and there are many, that the more experienced we get the more set-ups we see that can trick us into getting out of positions early.

What do I mean by a set-up?

Easy. You're watching a gap, for example, close nicely, as expected, and you are almost counting your winnings. Suddenly, the market reverses and goes the wrong way. Oops! You watch your precious profits being eroded. You were £200 up and you watch that drop to £180, £170, £160, £150 …

Suddenly you become convinced that the market will continue to move against you and you'll lose the rest of the money you have made in that trade. Time to bail out, you reason to yourself!

You jump ship with, say, a 15 point profit (say £150). Phew! At least you've salvaged something.

But wait!

You look on in horror as the market suddenly reverses again and quickly closes the gap. Damn! That would have been 60 points in the bag, but you settled for 15.

What made you jump ship may be a set-up, meaning a trading signal that you have used in the past, but in this case it is not useful, as it just tricks you out of trades. Of course sometimes you get rewarded for this bad trading behaviour, which is where random reinforcement comes in.

This is a temptation to avoid and it is much easier for the inexperienced to get suckered like this. The experienced may see more set-ups but they also know what they should be doing (i.e. staying with it). Let me explain this in more detail.

Typically a new trader finds books to read, internet articles to digest and different traders to follow. Also typically he will experiment with a number of different techniques and systems and then dispense with each as they produce a number of consecutive losses. *This is complete foolishness as all systems will produce a number of consecutive losses from time to time.*

Whilst this process is going on there will be a tendency to lose money and this affects confidence. It is at this point that a trader is likely to start placing stops too tightly (because he is frightened of losing more money) and grab profits too early (because he is desperate for a profit, *any* profit, even one that is far too small).

Plus traders will pick up random bits of knowledge, which may be called experience, and will start seeing patterns which they *think* mean the market will do x when they see y.

This is very dangerous when you need to run profits. You will keep seeing signs suggesting the move will not continue in your favour and tempting you to bail out early.

And do you know the very worst thing that can happen to you?

It is if you are proven right!

You see this sign and get this gut feeling that you should bail out – and so you do. To your intense satisfaction you note that you were correct and the market moves sharply against you. Phew! You would have lost 52 points if you'd stuck with that turkey!

Unfortunately now you are in a desperate situation. You believe you have secret insight and mystical intuition not given to mere mortals. From that day on you will go by your gut feeling when to exit a market – and that will often be too early.

If you do that you will just spin your wheels and never make any progress. You need to hardwire the concept and importance of *running profits* so that you do not get seduced into doing the opposite.

There's a conspiracy against you

When you have traded for long enough, and been taken out often enough by a stop which is too tight, you may come to believe that the market is against you; that there is some sort of conspiracy against you, personally; that they are out to get you. It just seems uncanny.

The market takes you out time after time, then happily sails away into profit land, leaving you to watch on the sidelines. It doesn't seem fair.

I believe there are two factors at work here. One is the market genuinely *is* against you (but not you personally, just every fool who places stops too tightly). And there is a psychological component too.

Let's take the psychological component first.

The psychology

One of the reasons we keep meticulous records of our trades is because we humans are total rubbish at objectively remembering our wins and losses. I've lost count of the number of people who tell me they are in profit with their share portfolio, but have a drawer full of losing shares which they don't count.

We can also rapidly get into negative magical thinking along these lines:

> "Whenever I set a stop too tight I *always* just get taken out. It's not fair!"

Actually, if you kept records, you may find this only happens, say, 50% of the time. It's just that the gross unfairness of it lives large in your memory because it has a powerful emotional tag associated with it. It's similar to saying "The other kids *always* pick on me", or "Women *always* turn me down when I ask for a dance", when these things only happen sometimes.

Similarly we can get into positive magical thinking:

> "Whenever I see 8 followed by 24 at the casino, then 11 always comes up and I've *always* cleaned up on this combination."

Actually this only happened once and *nearly* happened a second time (you were *that* close …), but you were so thrilled to win that first time that you started to believe in this combination.

With trading it's the easiest thing in the world to start to believe that a certain pattern *always* results in a sign for you to get in or out of a trade. In fact this only proved correct once or twice but you have a powerful and positive emotional tag attached to that pattern.

Psychologically, words like 'always', 'never' and 'every' are known as *generalisations* and can be a useful way for the mind to take shortcuts in processing. Unfortunately, generalising a few successful bad-habit trades doesn't mean it will always work in your favour. Worse still, using words that generalise experiences creates a 'there are no exceptions and therefore there are no choices' mentality which puts blinkers on your thinking.

The best traders I know are fairly unemotional in their trading. They don't care that much if they win (hence they can let profits run). They care a bit more if they lose (hence they cut their losses with a wide-ish stop).

Conversely, the worst traders (and they don't last long) are those who are emotional about trades and engage in magical thinking of the sort I have described.

You may think that you will never succumb to these problems; that you are above such primitivism. Don't be too sure! Perhaps you're reading this believing that you are quite capable of following a few simple rules, mechanically, and just banking the cash, thank you very much.

Oh yeah?

Come back when you've done this for six months and I'd be astonished if you hadn't made some terrible decisions which are nothing to do with what I've been teaching you.

This is the sort of thing I mean:

1. **Bailing out early** because you just knew the market was going to turn against you. (Remember, the worst thing that can happen here is that it does!)

2. **Not setting a stop** (you are playing Russian roulette with your total trading pot and inviting wipe-out).

3. **Setting tighter stops** because you are frightened.

4. Horror of horrors, starting to **take trades which have nothing to do with your system** because you intuitively feel that the market is going to rise (or fall). The worst thing that can happen here is that you are proved right.

5. Significantly **increasing or decreasing the amount you bet on a trade** because you just feel that this is the big one, or that this is not a great trade. You know what's coming! Again, the worst thing that can happen is that you are proved to be correct.

I firmly believe it is this list which makes the difference between a winner and a loser in trading.

It is the ability to rise above our natural (and utterly fallible) human instincts and emotions which sorts the men out from the boys.

In other words, successful trading is less about the system and more about taming and training your mind. This is why, of course, wannabe traders meander from system to system hoping for the Holy Grail when all along the problem is there between their ears. Just look in a mirror and you will see what I am talking about.

Now read through those five items above once more. Hear what I am saying. Master those five points and you will make it.

Is that so tough?

I'll have a lot more to say about trading psychology as we progress as it is critical to your success.

You're not paranoid

Let's now have a quick look at the second factor which makes you think the markets are all out to get you.

It's because … *they are*!

Not you, personally, you understand (although it feels that way). It's just that the market comprises millions of separate intelligences all vying against each other. As such, it can seem sometimes like a single alive entity (in the same way that a mob can seem like a single, organic entity with its own intelligence, will and desire).

Here are the shenanigans which this entity called the market indulges in:

- It regularly **breaches resistance lines**, suckers a load of traders into taking an up bet, then promptly crashes back down through the resistance line and wipes them all out.

- It regularly **drops through support lines**, suckers a load of traders into taking a down bet, then promptly soars back up through the support line and wipes them all out.

- And … it frequently **tests stops which are too tight**. It sniffs them out, nudges up against them, goes one millionth of a percent the other side (I exaggerate, naturally, even though I've told people a million times I never exaggerate) and takes the stop out, only to immediately reverse and move into positive territory once again leaving thousands of furious punters screaming at their screens!

Bear in mind that the job of the market is to maximise trade. Merely placing a stop is an order to trade and if the market can hit that stop it will. This is why stops close to market action are so vulnerable. The market, meaning the more experienced traders, *know* where the less experienced place stops and they seek them out – hence we place stops beyond their grasp, at least beyond their usual grasp.

I confess I don't know precisely *how* the market does this, but trust me it does. The market has an uncanny, almost infallible nose for too tight a stop and this is why my wider stops give you a real market advantage.

This does not mean you cannot place stops close to the action, but if you do you need to be working in a short time frame – perhaps working with 1-minute and 5-minute trading charts. If your trading plan involves bigger swing trades then you have to use wider stops and give the trade room to breathe.

We now turn our attention to Money Management.

Section 3 –
Money Management

PURPOSE OF MONEY MANAGEMENT

THE FIRST ROLE OF MONEY MANAGEMENT (MM) IS TO KEEP YOUR cash safe. This serves three distinct purposes:

1. It means you do not get wiped out so you have the time to learn the life skill of trading markets. I can give you all the theory you need but a vital aspect of success is all about the psychology involved and this only comes into play when you trade for real.

2. Recovering money is difficult psychologically and practically. For example, if you lost 90% you would have to multiply the remaining 10% nine times to recover – a very formidable task! Even losing 50% is too much, as you then have to double the remaining 50%.

3. Once you understand this you can increase your stake (the amount you trade per point) and that is when you really start to make decent amounts of money.

To explain the first of the above consider two facts. The first is that many trading systems have a 50% hit rate and the second is that a 50% hit rate gives an expectation of strings of 10 or 11 losses every 1000 trades. Although the normal expectation is a string of 10 or 11 losses, over time you would see every variation and there could be strings of 20 or 30 losses – 1000 losses in a row would be a very, very long shot!

Assuming the normal expectation and if you were to risk 10% of your pot on every trade you would thus be wiped out every 1000 trades as that nasty string of losses came along. OK, you would expect this to take some time, but these strings of losses can come at any time – they could be your first ten trades!

You would also expect strings of 10 or 11 winners in a row, but nobody complains about those.

So 10% is too much for any one bet, even though you would, in any case, use 10% *of the reducing balance* with each trade, meaning you would always have 90% left.

Standard trading wisdom is to risk between 2% and 4% of your pot on any one trade. This may seem a very small amount but bear in mind that:

- There is no rush. The key advantage you have is that time is on your side – get this right and money will start to roll in quickly enough to suit anyone.

- If you risk too much too quickly you can end up giving yourself too much pain and this can set you up psychologically in totally the wrong way.

The risk of 2% to 4% makes a lot of sense when you consider those strings of 10 or 11 losers. At 4% you could be down 40% which is quite enough, thank you very much! If each loss were exactly 4%, ten losses in a row would actually produce an overall loss of 35% of your original capital as each time you risk 4% it is on the reducing balance.

My suggestion is to translate the percentages into a simple approach which I find works very well in practice: **trade pounds per point equal to how many thousands of pounds you have in your trading account.**

So let's say you start with £1,000 in the account – you trade £1 per point – once you have doubled to £2,000 you trade £2 per point, etc., etc.

That is my base MM system and if we take a system which conveniently uses a maximum stop of 40 points we find that at £1 per point this is equal to £40. If we are trading with £1000 that equals 4%; and if we stick to £1 per point up to £1999 that percentage drops to 2.6% – well within the band.

Resist the temptation to vary from this rule in the first few months of trading. Later as your experience develops you are free to use your own judgement.

There is also no reason why you should not start with a lower sum than £1,000, but you may find the minimum betting sizes a problem. With IG Index the minimum is usually £2 per point, but other companies have lower minimums.

All these figures will need to be revised by those who use exchange-traded futures contracts in the UK, US or worldwide.

If you use much tighter stops then the £1 per £1000 rule does not apply, but it does depend on what you are trying to achieve in the market. Tight stops tend not to work if you are trying to run positions to make bigger profits.

An experienced trader will make up his or her own rules and, in this context, may see any system as a starting point – a canvas upon which to create their own successful trading personality, possibly involving multiple markets and multiple systems. Certainly all the successful traders I know do this.

Incidentally, when using trading robots which will trade mechanically on your behalf you can usually set the risk level as a percentage of account size. This means that each trade is automatically adjusted as winners and losers come in. However, many private traders do not even consider this. They tend to stick to so many pounds per point even when using different stop points and risk levels. For this reason their Money Management is all over the place.

The basic rules are straightforward, but it is possible to go a lot further; for example, to aggressively bump up trading size as winners come in and to do the opposite as losers add up. However this is complex and also very dependent on your trading results.

This is advanced stuff and is a step no one should take until they have the basics down pat – do not try to run before you can walk! So trade a basic system for a while until you feel you thoroughly understand it.

A word of caution

Now we are delving into areas which are more complex and so, as I said above, make sure you have the basics down pat before you venture into these advanced areas.

Do not even think of employing the techniques in this section until you have a steadily increasing bank balance following the basic methodology of your system.

What follows may be a bit difficult to understand at first. You will need to carefully read these ideas several times over until you get it.

Finally I want to say a word about size. The techniques in this section are all about increasing size once you hit a string of winners. If you are already trading in size this may impact on you psychologically. You need to be sure you will be comfortable trading at these increased levels. If you are very happy at your current level of size then do not change this for the sake of it.

HOW TO INCREASE PROFITS AND REDUCE LOSSES

Supposing there was a way of ramping up the cash you earn from your winners whilst correspondingly cutting your losses even further?

Does that sound good?

I think so!

But – and there is always a but with these things – whatever technique we employ in the markets there will be some sequences of profits and losses which really suit that technique, and others that make us pay for employing it.

It is important to realise that once you apply rigid discipline to your trading by using a system, the way the market behaves directly affects your profits and losses. In this fashion the market can be seen as a *generator of random sequences* and, over time, it will run through the full range of such sequences. This is why I say some traders are fugitives from the law of averages in the sense that their strategies are flawed and one day the market will generate the sequence that will expose those flaws and wipe them out.

Getting back to our strategy for ramping up profits, let me illustrate this by way of three MM systems.

MM System One

Here is a simple MM approach designed to maximise profits:

we simply double our stake on each successive win.

Note: I am *not* recommending you do this, as we will see.

We start with £1 per point. If we win, we then go to £2 per point. A further win and we are on £4 per point, then £8 per point and so on and so on.

The table below shows how profits will ramp up if you begin with six winning trades in a row and assuming 20 points profit per trade.

Trade	Result	Profit
1	£2 pp × 20 points	£40
2	£4 pp × 20 points	£80
3	£8 pp × 20 points	£160
4	£16 pp × 20 points	£320
5	£32 pp × 20 points	£640
6	£64 pp × 20 points	£1280

Wow, what a system!

We have now banked £2520 of profit over just six trades and we are really rolling!

We are rubbing our hands in anticipation of the next win, which would make us a tasty £2560 in a single trade when …

Trade 7: £128 pp × -52 points = £6656 LOSS!!

Oops!

The trade went against us and we got stopped out with our standard 52 point stop (this example is based on *ZeitGap*).

It turns out this approach has a fatal flaw: as soon as the system hits a 52 point loss (our standard stop loss) we lose all we have made, *plus* a lot more besides.

You almost certainly expected this result as this is one of the most basic systems around for amplifying gains.

So, back to the drawing board.

For the next system, we use something similar to before, but clearly we need to be a little more subtle.

MM System Two

This time we will not double our stake on each successive win. Instead we will use a formula based on the last profit we made – we will bet a little extra depending on the magnitude of the previous win.

To calculate this, we will divide the number of pounds won in the previous trade by 50, halve the result and add this to the size of our bet. We divide by 50 as 52 is our maximum possible loss (subject to slippage) and so we use 50 to make it simpler. We then halve the result so that we are only risking half of that previous profit. To make it even easier just divide by 100 which gives the same result.

A couple of examples should help you to understand what we are doing:

1. We previously **won £90 betting £2 a point**. Dividing this by 50 gives 1.8. Halving this gives 0.9. (Dividing by 100 gives exactly the same result.) So we increase our bet by 90p. We bet £2.90 next time. In practice we might bet £3.

2. We previously **won £150 betting £5 a point**. Dividing this by 50 gives 3. Halving this gives 1.5. So we increase our bet by £1.50 and bet £6.50 next time.

This way, if we *do* get stopped out we will never lose more than half of the prior profit in addition to the normal loss. Remember, in the doubling system we could lose *all* our prior profit. This system aims to prevent that.

This needs a little explaining so let's take the second example from above.

Bet 1: We win £150 at £5/pt

So, according to our system, we bet £6.50/pt on the next trade. So let's do that …

Bet 2: £6.50/pt

For ease of understanding, think of this as a bet of £5/pt (our original stake) and an extra bet of £1.50/pt (risking half of our previous profit). If this *second* part of our trade goes wrong and we get stopped out for 52 points, we'd lose 52 × £1.50 = £78 which is about half of our previous £150 win.

Supposing we lose the maximum on the next trade, which is 52 pts.

Our losses are thus:

£5 × 52 = £260. Plus £1.50 × 52 = £78.

Looking again at that £78, you can see it is about half of the previous £150 profit – so *we only risked half of the profit we made previously, by having this extra £1.50 bet.*

Let's see how this works with real data.

This time I am going to vary the profits in line with actual trading results (the data comes from how *ZeitGap* performed in May 2012). The data is shown in the following table.

Let me first explain the column headings in the table:

- *Date:* This one's obvious I hope – it's the date we took the trade.

- *Entry:* The figures in this column show the point at which we entered the market. *ZeitGap* waits for the first 5-minute bar to completely form. Then we wait for a 2 point move above (or below) the high (or low) of that 5-minute bar in the direction of closing the gap. This is our confirmation signal. The figure in this column shows what that level was. S means we sold the market (looking to close the gap in the downward direction) and B means we bought the market (looking to close the gap in the upward direction).

- *Exit:* This is the point at which we are looking to exit the trade. This is nominally the previous closing level, but we add or subtract a 2 pt safety margin. If we want to close the gap in the downward direction, we add 2 pts to the previous close (i.e. get out just before the gap closes). If we want to close the gap in the upward direction, we subtract 2 pts from the previous close (i.e. we get out just before the gap closes). The calculation shows the size of the gap we are trading. For example, on 2 May we had a 94 point gap.

- *Max loss on the day:* This doesn't mean we lost this amount! It's the maximum excursion into negative territory that the index made during the day, meaning how far it went against our position.

- *Profit:* If we made a profit it will be shown here as a positive figure. If we made a loss it will be shown here as a negative figure. Our maximum loss, due to our 52 point stop, is -52 points. So on 2 May, we made 94 points. On 14 May we were stopped out for a loss of -52 points.

Date	Entry	Exit	Max loss on day	Profit
2 May	S 6857	6763	-10	+94
3 May	S 6846 triggered 14h45!!	6712	-10 or less	+34
4 May	B 6682	6692		
7 May	B 6427	6559		+132
8 May	B 6554	6567		+13
9 May	S 6474	6446		+28
10 May	S 6523	6477		+46
11 May	B 6476	6516		+40
14 May	B 6509	6579		-52
15 May	S 6493 (6486)	6453		+40
16 May	B 6347 (6347)	6399		+42
17 May	S 6389 (6389)	6386		
18 May	B 6258 (6260)	6306		+50
21 May	O 6269 (6264)	6271	Ignore	
22 May	S 6377 (6370)	6333		-22
23 May	B 6357 (5359)	6433	11 stop 6321	-36
24 May	S 6335 (6334)	6287		+48

Date	Entry	Exit	Max loss on day	Profit
25 May	S 6332 (6323)	6317		+15
28 May	S 6414 (6398)	6341		+73
29 May	S 6392 (6375)	6325		+29
30 May	B 6369 (6368)	6394		0
31 May	S 6284 (6284)	6282	<11 ignore	
MAY 2012 RESULTS	Days: 22 Ignore:4	W: 14L: 3b/e: 1	+686-110	+576

Note: the system in May 2012 had an 82% hit rate.

Let's look at how our second MM system fares. Remember we *increase* the bet by the formula after every winning bet (incidentally, we will be looking at what we do when we lose later). To calculate the revised trading size I have simply divided the profit by 100 and added the result to the previous size, rounding to whole numbers where I consider it useful.

Date	Result	Profit	Comment
02-May	£2 pp × 94 pts	£188	New bet size is £3.80. We will round this down to £3.50 as some spread betting companies only use 50p increments. To keep the sums simple I have also rounded to whole numbers of pounds for the later trades.
03-May	£3.50 pp × 34 pts	£119	New bet size is £4.50. (£119 divided by 100 is £1.19 so we increase our bet by £1.19. This gives a new bet of £4.69 which we round to £4.50.)
07-May	£4.50 pp × 132 pts	£594	New bet size is £10.00
08-May	£10 pp × 13 pts	£130	New bet size is £11.00

Date	Result	Profit	Comment
09-May	£11 pp × 28 pts	£308	New bet size is £14.00
10-May	£14 pp × 46 pts	£644	New bet size is £20.00
11-May	£20 pp × 40 pts	£800	New bet size is £28.00
14-May	£28 pp × -52 pts	-£1,456	

We have won £2595 and lost £1456, which leaves us £1139 in profit.

So, this is a distinct improvement, but that £1456 loss still managed to eliminate the *previous two profits* (£800 + £644). The problem is that we *always* lose at the highest number of £s per point because we are gradually increasing our stake.

We can categorise trading systems into two broad groups:

1. The first group have bigger profits than losses but tend to have a hit rate (meaning the percentage of winning trades) at around 50% or less. In simple terms, they lose steadily and often but when they win, they win big.

2. The second group have a much higher hit rate but the size of an individual loss *can* exceed the size of the average profit.

Gap systems (like *ZeitGap*) tend to fall into the second grouping; this is important as the higher hit rate makes it much easier to trade. This is because traders do not like losses and especially strings of losses. The higher hit rate largely makes the trading experience far more enjoyable. But that occasional large loss (e.g. 52 points) causes a difficulty when we try to really ramp up our gains.

So here is a solution, provided by MM System Three.

MM System Three

We vary the system and use a tighter stop than our standard 52 points *for the extra part of our trade* in which we are trying to ramp up our profits. This changes the dynamics of the risk/reward and the revised system will now fall into the first grouping of trading systems given above.

This is how it works: we use the first 5-minute bar of the session to trigger our trade and we revise our stop policy for the extra part of our trade to 5 points beyond the other extreme of that first 5-minute bar.

- If we **buy** the market our stop (for this second part of the trade remember) is now 5 points below the low of the first 5-minute bar.

- If we **sell** the stop is 5 points above the high of the first 5-minute bar.

Now, you will recall my exhortations earlier about keeping stops relaxed and you may, quite rightly, see this approach as flying in the face of that.

Well it does so!

But it is not the whole story because we mix and match, we stick with our standard system (the 52 point stop) for the main part of the bet but we *also* look to bag bigger profits using the approach with the tighter stop for the other part of our bet.

In other words, we are effectively going to be making *two* bets each time. One using the standard 52 point stop and a second trying to bag larger profits with this tighter stop to take advantage of a series of wins.

What is the logic of this?

The logic of this is that there are times when a system like *ZeitGap* is on fire, gaps being closed in every direction, and this is the time when the extra bet with the tighter stop may prove highly profitable.

But there are other times when volatility is low and this can be a bad time for the system – the summer holiday months are one example, as is December when everything tends to fall asleep. These are times when you may prefer to keep your trading down to a minimum.

The basic idea of this new dual bet/tighter stop approach is that:

1. The main *ZeitGap* system will still be in place (**bet one**) and so you could still win overall, even if the shorter-term stop gets taken out.

2. Meanwhile we have a nice little side bet (**bet two**) with part of our position using this tighter stop. If that comes good, we can bag lots of extra points.

To achieve this we aim for the same £s per point on both parts of the position.

So let me just spell this out.

In this new system we effectively take *two bets at a time* if a trade is triggered. Looking at *ZeitGap* these two bets are:

*   **Bet 1***:* Our standard *ZeitGap* bet, as you have learned so far, with a nice wide 52-point stop. There's no difference there from what you've been doing so far.

*   **Bet 2***:* Another bet *of the same size*, but with a tighter stop based on the first 5-minute bar as we have discussed.

We are now going to apply this new idea to the trades in May. I will explain how I suggest you do this as I go along.

Remember these are advanced techniques so don't expect just to get this in one reading! It is not a problem if you are confused at this point, but as you read and reread what I have written I'm hoping it will all become clear. There are some diagrams later to help you understand.

The formula

We are going to make a split bet (two bets) of equal amounts (i.e. £2 + £2 per point).

To calculate how many pounds per point we bet (e.g. £2 in the above example) *after a win*, we use this formula:

1. Take the previous profit and halve it.

2. Divide it by the total risk for the next bet (I'll calculate this for you in a moment).

3. This gives (rounded) the number of pounds per point to allocate to each half of the next bet and, remember, we bet the same amount on each half.

How do we calculate the total risk?

Well, it's a two-part bet. One part is our standard *ZeitGap* bet with its maximum 52 point risk. So that's easy. The second part is a little more complex to calculate because it's based on our new, tighter stop which is 5 points beyond the H (or L) of the first 5-minute bar.

Imagine the first 5-minute bar is 10 points long and we are placing an UP bet. We know our entry level is 2 points above the top of this bar. We know our new tighter stop must be 5 points below the bottom of this bar. So our risk (on this half of the bet) is 10 + 2 + 5 = 17 points. Putting it simply, if this part of our trade was stopped out, we'd lose 17 points.

The following diagram should make this clear. The principle is the same whether we are taking an UP bet or a DOWN bet.

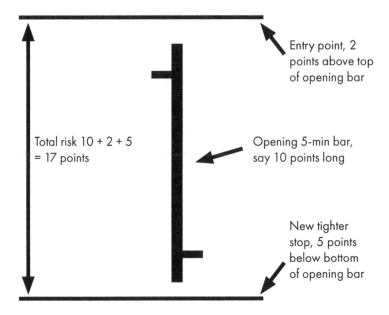

Entry point, 2 points above top of opening bar

Total risk 10 + 2 + 5 = 17 points

Opening 5-min bar, say 10 points long

New tighter stop, 5 points below bottom of opening bar

So in this example our *total* risk is:

- 52 on bet 1
- 17 on bet 2

which together give a total risk of 69 points (52 + 17).

Let's see how we calculate this in a worked example from May:

TRADE 1, May 2: £2 pp × 94 points = £188 PROFIT

No change to trade 1 as it is the first in the sequence.

We now apply our formula to work out the next bet.

We have £188 profit divided by 2 = £94 to allocate between the two parts of the next trade: our standard *ZeitGap* trade and our more aggressive trade with the tighter stop.

Why divided by 2?

Remember, it's because we don't want to risk more than half of the previous profit.

We now need to work out our tighter stop for the second part of the trade. In this case the first 5-minute bar was 16 points long so our stop is 23 points (16 + 5 +2 = 23).

Our total risk is therefore 52 + 23 = 75 points.

At this point we need to equalise the two halves of the bet (and this only applies the first time we ramp up) so the first step is to allocate £2 per point to the part of the bet with the tighter stop. £2 per point × 23 pips = £46. If we then take £46 from £94 we are left with £48 which is only enough for an additional 50p on each bet and I have ignored this to keep it simpler.

We now divide £94 by 75 and ...

TRADE 2, May 3: £2 + £2 pp × 34 points = £136 PROFIT

This calculation is slightly more complex as we have to work out the tighter stop. In this case the first 5-minute bar was 16 points long so our stop is 23 points (16 + 5 +2 = 23). In this case we add an additional £2 per point on the tighter-stop part of the trade.

NB As the stop is tighter you can add more to that part if desired as you are risking less. I have rounded down to give £2 + £2 in trade 2.

TRADE 3, May 7: £3 + £3 pp × 132 points = £792 PROFIT

For trade 4 the first 5-minute bar was only 7 points long so our stop is 14 points away from our entry allowing us to increase the trading size more aggressively and we have £396 (£792 divided by 2 = £396) to split for trade 4.

Again the DAX never looked back after triggering the trade quite late in the session so both parts were winners.

TRADE 4, May 8: £9 + £9 pp × 13 points = £234 PROFIT

Another winner for both parts, and for trade 5 the 5-min bar is 14 points long, so our stop is 21 points away.

TRADE 5, May 9: £11 + £11 pp × 28 points = £616 PROFIT

Yet again both parts win and the 5-minute bar for trade 6 is only 6 points deep, so the stop is 13 points.

TRADE 6, May 10: £16 + £16 pp × 46/-13 points = £528 PROFIT

The tighter stop got hit this time. About time too! But we still made money. For trade 7 the bar is 12 points so stops are 19 points.

TRADE 7, May 11: £19 +£19 pp × 40 points = £1520 PROFIT

The DAX missed the tighter stop by only 2 points but both parts win. For trade 8 the 5-min bar is 10 points wide, so stop is 17 points.

TRADE 8, May 14: £24 + £24 pp × -52/-17 points = £1656 LOSS

OK, we knew it was coming! But note we have a two-part trade. We lose £24 pp on our 52 point stop = £1248. We also lose £24 pp × 17 = £408 on our tighter 17 point stop on that part of the trade. The total loss is £1656.

NB To calculate the revised trading size I have simply divided half the previous profit by 52 + the tighter stop and added the result to the previous size.

Now the odds mean that every successive profit is less likely as the string gets longer and longer, *but* each independent result has the same probability as usual.

Nevertheless you may feel it is worthwhile to be more cautious after the third/fourth/fifth trade and become less aggressive.

You may also want to look at the total risk you are taking on each new trade and consider this in the light of the profits you have made so far. Using this sort of system there will always be a trade-off between the larger potential profits and the risks being taken and as you develop your expertise you will make decisions that suit your style of trading.

The key point to focus on is the importance of making lots of hay whilst the sun shines and this is what this section is all about.

WHAT TO DO WITH LOSSES

The nature of *ZeitGap* means we tend to get better strings of wins but smaller strings of losses – in fact I have just checked five months' worth of my trading records and we only had two occasions where there were two losses in a row; there were no strings of three or more losses.

The drawback with aggressively reducing your stake size as losses come in is the inverse of the problem of losing with the highest stake we came across with winners – we always win with the lowest stake.

So my suggestion is to let the standard Money Management rules deal with the losses. By that I mean we start back at the beginning once a loss occurs. Press *reset* if you like.

Section 4 – Your Psychology Techniques

PSYCHOLOGY IS A TECHNIQUE

PSYCHOLOGY IS THE THIRD OF OUR THREE KEY FACTORS WHICH make the difference between a successful trader and one who steadily loses money.

You may think it odd to call our own psychology a technique, but I think it is because, for example, winners will do what it takes to make a success of their lives and losers will not. This is a fairly fundamental difference and, ultimately, we can choose which of these techniques we prefer.

Having said that, often no choice is involved. Winners simply develop winning habits and losers develop losing habits.

Just realising we have that choice can be a *big* step forward and many seem trapped in the false belief that they have no choice in this key matter. It is important to realise that we each hold a multitude of beliefs and that a great many of them are false; this especially applies to the negative beliefs we have about ourselves.

Here is a simple exercise used by, the sadly late, Zig Ziglar, previously one of the top life coaches in the world. He liked to talk about seeing *opportunity* in the context of this group of letters ...

NOWHERE

The winner will look for opportunity and find it is NOW! HERE! But the loser will see that opportunity is NOWHERE.

Okay, a bit corny, but it does make the distinction about seeing life as a series of great opportunities, or seeing it as a series of negatives and obstacles.

CHOOSE TO BE A WINNER

I know people who are winners and they get out and do things despite the setbacks. They have learned an important life lesson: the more you do, the more you learn, and your increasing knowledge makes you more able to see the best opportunities and capitalise on them.

I also know people who *choose* to be losers and as opportunity is nowhere (according to them) they never do anything, never learn anything, and never get anywhere.

They are constantly framing life in terms of why they *can't* do something, rather than why they can.

Success coach, Les Meehan, has a useful reframe similar to that of Zig Ziglar mentioned above. When you think something is:

IMPOSSIBLE

Add two little changes so it says:

I'M POSSIBLE

It is important to always have an 'I'm Possible' mindset to overcome challenges and not let them defeat you.

Some time ago I sent a link to a video clip to someone who was struggling, as I thought it would help his failing business. His response was that his computer had broken down and it was clear he saw this as an insurmountable problem, certainly sufficient for him to take no further action to repair it and get back on track.

His computer breakdown made it 'Impossible' to do anything!

I thought to myself "Here is a member of the dominant species on this planet, a species that has made this planet its own, has built huge cities, explored areas of space and the oceans, discovered huge amounts of knowledge, created great art, made giant strides in every direction, yet this miracle of biology sees this absolutely trivial problem as one to completely stop him in his tracks!"

Given ten minutes or less I could come up with at least 20 easy solutions to this problem – including a visit to the local internet café.

I think we all know people like that, but I cannot imagine any of us want to be like that ourselves, at least not for any length of time.

My belief is we can *choose* how we want to see and interact with the world. If we find that our current approach is not giving us what we want then due to our amazing adaptability we are able to make changes and hone in on the target.

Certainly I do this myself and I find the key is simply *to do something*; pretty much anything will do with the only caveat being that it needs to have some positive potential (that negative potential needs to be minimised goes without saying).

ACTION STARTS THE LEARNING/ EARNING HABIT

Once you stop talking and start to take serious action the world will grant you the greatest of its gifts. Some people call this gift failure and, for reasons I have trouble understanding, it carries a negative connotation.

But when something you do fails to produce the desired result that is when you learn the most and this is when I find I make the most progress. The important point is that every time we get a result we don't want, it is an opportunity to learn and grow. Every bad result holds in it a seed of learning.

Now here's a little-known fact …

The successful and the wealthy fail *more often* than losers and the poor because they are always pushing their boundaries.

Putting it simply, if you try once and fail once then you have a 100% failure rate. If you try 20 times and fail five times you've had four more failures than the first person, but a 75% success rate!

As far as I am concerned, if I don't fail at least once every week I am not trying hard enough – once a day is better.

The truth is if you want to increase your successes, the easiest way is to increase the number of your failures. Richard Denny said that first and it is *very* true.

The difference is that successful, wealthy people see failure for what it is – a gift to point the way to eventual success – whereas losers let it stop them in their tracks and they often never get going again.

So that is one key element of what I am calling the **trading psychology technique**.

YOU NEED MORE THAN JUST A SYSTEM

With the systems I develop for my clients I do all the hard work, I develop and test out the system and then present it as clearly as I know how. It is then up to you to put it to use in your own life and start making it work to bring in steady trading profits.

I mention this as I know many traders have trouble developing their own systems. As I said before I believe a system is essential, plus in the early years a trader will not know enough to develop their own systems.

Once they have the experience, I am a strong advocate that traders should develop their own market approach, but they need to develop that experience and a system helps a lot with this process.

Trading markets is never a completely straightforward process and you will encounter setbacks (failures if you like); you need to see these as the learning opportunities they are and not be distracted from your final goal.

I know that many beginner traders are not all that keen to learn about psychology. They see it as unnecessary, that is if they notice it at all. They believe the important thing is to have a killer system which they can follow.

In fact there is some truth in that view, a killer system is important, but if you fall into that category you are in for a rude awakening once you start trading for real.

If you've done some trading already, you won't need me to tell you about the importance of psychology. You see, we are not emotionless Mr Spocks. We are powerfully emotional creatures and when trading it is a challenge to stop strong emotions washing over us in strong waves:

- waves of exhilaration and feelings of omnipotence when our trading is going well,
- waves of depression and crushing feelings of unfairness when our trading goes against us.

What marks out successful traders is their ability to control their emotions in the trading situation.

It's not that they don't *have* emotions, it's just that they have taught themselves self-control.

A good example is being angry or upset at something which is totally out of your control. For example, feeling hard done by that it starts to rain on your washing.

I hope you can see there is absolutely nothing personal in it raining at that time. The rain gods don't know about your washing and it is not deliberate on their part. Therefore to feel aggrieved is utterly illogical.

You know what's coming ...

The markets are not sentient beings. But boy does it feel like they *are* sometimes! The markets are utterly disconnected from you, your petty worries, your desires, or the direction of your bet.

Remember, if you are losing on an up bet, someone else is winning because they took a down bet, so there's no agenda to the market.

But we humans have powerful and primitive tendencies to personalise non-sentient things. It's why primitive people believed in rock spirits and endowed talismans with powers. You may laugh, but scratch the surface and I promise you it's lurking just under your skin.

Just to clarify one point, I have said previously that the market breathes in and out, also that it is composed entirely of human beings and human psychology. These statements are true but are not inconsistent with the statement that the market is not sentient.

By this I mean the market, as such, does not have you in its sights. However, individual traders may do. They know where other traders tend to place stops and it can be part of a trading approach to hit such stops.

Whether they manage to do so will depend on how sensibly you have placed stops and what all the other traders do.

Now, the markets may be disconnected from you but you are part of that market and markets do exert strong psychological pulls, especially during strong trends. During such trends that psychological pull can be your friend (although you will tend to enter at non-optimal times), but the pull will be anything but your friend at key turning points!

What happens is that without discipline and training we start to personalise the market. We place a trade and immediately (to the nanosecond) the market moves against us:

"There! You see? Typical! The very second I place my trade the market sets out to take me out. It's just not fair!"

It's an unusual trader who hasn't felt like this at some point.

Now you're in trouble due to that thing many people airily dismiss: *psychology*. You are about to become an emo-trader. That's one who trades on emotion. They have another name in trading circles: losers.

What I'm saying is not unique to trading. Many people make lots of money playing professional poker. It is not luck that you win at poker.

How do I know that?

Because the same names win year after year in the big tournaments so it can't be total luck (there is an element of luck, naturally, just as there is with trading).

People think poker players are unemotional and hard-nosed. They miss the point:

Poker players are only unemotional and hard-nosed at the poker table.

They have trained themselves not to feel emotional when playing.

Why?

Because emotional decisions are bad and if they make emotional decisions they will lose.

How about you? Do you want to win?

To do that you're going to need more than a winning system. You need to pay attention to your psychology.

You need to learn discipline. You need to train yourself not to get emotional when trading, and to walk away from trading for a while the second you feel your emotions rising.

That's the secret winning edge which top traders have and many amateur traders don't have.

It's exactly the same problem with winning by the way. Once you start winning another very dangerous human emotion kicks in. It's called delusional omnipotence.

You start to imagine that you are special; that you've really nailed this trading malarkey due to your superior intellect and skills. Nobody can touch you. You're the man (or the woman).

Pretty soon you're taking trades which form no part of your trading plan, riding high on your supernatural abilities and awesome omniscience. As I said before, the very worst thing that can happen to you now is that you win! All that does is cement in place your feelings of invulnerability.

You are heading for a big and painful fall. It's called *wipeout*.

By the way, I've never met a trader who didn't get wiped out at some point in their career. Including me.

The trick is to use that as a sharp wake-up call.

Of course, many abandon trading at that point and that may be the right decision – trading is most definitely not for everyone. But it is those who carry on regardless who reap the big rewards. As I said earlier it is all about choice: your choice.

REMEMBER THIS ...

Put the following on a 3 × 5 card and keep it close to you:

- You DON'T have special powers not given to other mere mortals.

- You are NOT a great trader (but you can work at being a good one).

- The market is NOT against you personally.

- Many trades WILL go against you.

- You WILL get stopped out by just one point from time to time only to see the market soar away in a winning direction after it's dumped you by the side of the road.

- You WILL have ridiculously lucky breaks (you may say they are just luck but they are also a statistical certainty as long as your system is well grounded and you follow it including running the profits).

- You WILL have annoying losing streaks (ditto as above, except you may call these bad luck).

- STICK WITH YOUR SYSTEM. Don't place side bets.

THE MANIC DEPRESSIVE MODE

Many traders can become manic depressives. Becoming over-confident as the winners mount up only to suffer from hubris and to abandon the very rules that gave them that success. They then make reckless gambles based on nothing more than a feeling of euphoria. Losses then come in and they sink into depression and start to trade fearfully. They feel that everyone is against them. They start catastrophising – that's when we exaggerate the normal slings and arrows of life:

"It's always the same, I never win."

"They'll make sure I can't get ahead."

"It's not fair."

"Why me?"

At the time this can be quite subtle and the trader can be so wrapped up with their own internal emotional landscape and the market action that they cannot see what is really going on.

It is very well known that emotions make us temporarily stupid. It's the fact that lies behind the saying 'love is blind', for example.

But emotions have *evolved* to make us stupid! They are fight or flight at the basic level. The organism doesn't have time for all that thinking nonsense. It's put 'em up, or run like hell.

Brain scans clearly show that when we are emotionally aroused, a crowbar is thrown across the circuits of the more rational parts of the brain.

We become incapable of thinking logically.

So you can see why emotions are a bad thing in the context of our trading.

If you find yourself becoming emotional (positive or negative) when trading, walk away then and there. The market will always be there when you return.

I want this to properly register in your mind; my aim is that you don't forget this in the heat of battle with the markets.

The manic depressive mode is just one example; this can last for years as a trader yo-yos between the two states achieving nothing of material value while he does so, and often steadily losing money.

You are unlikely to enter such extreme states in the first year or so as you learn the key experiential lessons of the trading arena. That's usually because you are not trading significant amounts of money. Things can change significantly when you have £50k riding on a trade. Try snapping your fingers at fate if you lose that amount; or try telling me you won't feel special if you win that amount!

The more aware you are of the tricks your psychology can play the better prepared you will be.

STRUCTURE OF THE BRAIN

Sometimes you are likely to find yourself thinking of taking a trade which has nothing to do with your system and you may wonder why. Many years ago this happened to me and I set about working it out. The answer may surprise you.

I'd had an argument with a friend earlier that day and I realised that this was why I had traded outside my system (what's called a self-justified, but essentially random, bet). Now that may seem bizarre but let me explain how it works out.

Human beings do a lot of stuff for emotional reasons (hold the front page!). Many of us may think we are entirely logical and sensible but this is far from the truth.

Psychologists divide the brain into three layered regions. This follows how the brain evolved over millions of years starting with the instinctive part, then the emotional part and finally the most recent thinking part.

As we evolved from the primeval swamp, or wherever it was we came from, these parts formed in turn. So the brain stem derives from our reptilian heritage and is millions of years old. This part provides our instinctive drives and automatic reactions to stimuli.

The next layer, called the limbic system, derives from our basic mammal heritage and involves emotional input. This too is very ancient.

Of more recent development is the neocortex, which involves reflective thought processes and imagination.

(This is a simplified picture and the subject is dealt with in more detail in *The Way to Trade*.)

The key problem

The problem is that trading triggers many *instinctive and emotional* reactions. These reactions put us into a certain physiological state

– defined simply as how you are thinking and feeling, but also including your body chemistry. These reactions are deeply buried within the functioning of our brains so it can be difficult for us to override them.

Although we are pleased to believe that we are rational creatures, the truth is a million miles from this. We are truly learner drivers of our three brains.

To me the mental contortions many of us go through when we want to buy a new car, for example, fully illustrate my point. Each of our three brains wants something different, so all kinds of different thoughts run through our heads.

Hence a basically simple activity, trading, can become very difficult to do well in practice when you are in the wrong physiological state.

After much thought I realised I had taken that bad trade because my self-esteem had taken a hit with the argument and this caused an emotional low.

I took the trade to feel good again.

In other words, I was in a negative state and my survival instincts wanted me back in a positive state, so my subconscious mind directed me to a trade that appeared to provide what I needed – a boost to my self-esteem!

Now think about this. One thing I have learnt by working with many other traders is how similar we all are. Faced with the same input, meaning the market and our trades, many of us will react in similar ways. There are variations but they tend to be within a fairly narrow band.

So, if I find myself taking a trade through a completely random factor beyond my conscious awareness, then it is likely you are prone to do the same.

One thing we can be sure of is that any such trade will have absolutely nothing to do with your carefully formulated trading plan. And remember, the worst thing that can happen is that it comes good!

It is not just arguments with friends you need to beware of; it can be far more subtle. Your physiological state changes all of the time and with the slightest internal or external stimulus. You can test this easily; remember a past negative experience and see how fast this changes how you feel. Now remember a very positive past experience and notice how you feel better again. This is state control.

It may be that you are interested in trading because you want a bit more fun in your life and want to keep active and alert – this is actually an extremely good reason and trading can be a very convenient, and profitable, way to do it.

Let's take the physiological state we call boredom …

You are bored, your mind and body are giving you clear messages of the state of boredom through your thoughts and feelings, and so you take action to alleviate this. Your subconscious wants you to feel better, it wants you to change your state. Makes sense, doesn't it? So what might you do if you get bored again?

Think about it.

You are liable to want to take a trade even if the system does not give a signal because at this point it is not about trading but about feeling better in yourself.

Now there are many ways in which our minds can trick us into trading when our system does not give us a signal, and you want to be on your guard for this.

- *The signal's nearly there … I'll get in early.*

- *I like the way this market is shaping up. I think I'll get in now.*

- *Wow! Interesting pattern! I bet the market's about to turn down. I think I'll have a punt on that.*

- *I wonder what would happen if I just …*

You may need a solution which does not involve trading. If so, find another activity which deals with the state issue. Maybe a short walk, a puzzle of some sort, a task you have been putting off – there are limitless things you could do instead of trading to change your state to one more conducive to trading.

There is only *one* reason to trade – ever:

> Your chosen system is sending a clear signal to enter or exit the market.

That's it. I told you trading was simple!

It's just *doing it* which people find so hard. And that's purely down to psychology and your state at that moment.

FIDDLING WITH THE TRADE SIZE

Here's another area which newbie (and some experienced) traders just cannot stop messing with: the size of the trade.

Again, my simple Money Management system clearly stipulates how much to risk (it's £1 per £1,000 we have in our trading pot). So if you're betting £2 a point you need a £2,000 trading bank.

An idiot could understand that instruction, but how often have I seen it broken? Countless times!

It's the same basic psychology at work here tinkering with the trading amount. Here are just three psychological factors (but there are many more):

1. Boredom

2. Omniscience

3. Fear

1. Boredom

You get weary of winning or losing £100 a time (or whatever) and you long for a bit of spice in your life. So just this once you'll pile in big time because the market is shaping up nicely for the big one.

This is a fast route to wipeout. If you lose, you may 'do a Leeson' and increase your bet next time to make up your losses.

You *cannot win* doing this.

Here's why …

If you double up and eventually *win*, that will just confirm your awesome powers, even though it was total dumb luck that you won. So that means you'll try the same crazy stunt again and again until you get wiped out.

Result from scenario #1 = WIPEOUT

If you *lose* you will rationalise your loss ("Oh, silly me, I hadn't noticed that the moon was in Leo and it was the 19th Thursday after Ascension Day – I'll be more careful next time."). The sting of the loss, coupled with your crazy rationalisations for why you lost, will provide an impossible to resist impetus to bet again (and bigger) to get your money back.

Result from scenario #2 = WIPEOUT

2. Omniscience

You believe you are something special. Way above mere mortals. A trading bank is for the plebs. You're a real Maverick – daring, cunning and clever. You're going to load on lots of money because you just know (with your secret powers) that this is going to be a *big* trade and it's exciting, an adrenaline rush that puts you in a high state.

3. Fear

You've been stung and are feeling in a weak and fearful state. Rather than continue with the size of bet which you should, you start to put way less on a trade, timidly hoping it will come good this time.

This fearful state is painful and you don't want to add to that pain so you trade without courage and confidence. If the trade loses, you are vindicated. You knew that trade was no good.

You're now heading for death by a thousand cuts as your trading pot is slowly whittled away to nothing.

This is clearly not a good state to be in for trading so walk away until you have regained your normal trading state.

CONCLUSION

I hope you have taken serious note of the critical importance of trading psychology and trading only when in the right physiological state. This is vital to your trading success.

In this section we have had no trading rules, but the subjects we have covered together here should prove of greater importance to you than any such rules.

You need a system, yes, but you also need the discipline to follow it. That means having a radar sense for when you are slipping into emotionality with its consequent short-circuiting of the rational mind. You can start to develop this radar sense by learning to become aware of your physiological states and how to control them.

Many traders destroy any hope of profits by taking many emotional trades. They even go so far as to abandon their system because it is not working!

This is our old friend catastrophising. It makes us think in absolutes. You get a small run of losses and so you say "This system *never* works!"

In fact the system is often fine, but the trader's emotions are hijacking his or her rational brain and they are simply in self-destruct mode, unable to face reality.

Watch out for this tendency and find something else to do when it comes up.

The road to success

There are not many careers which you can successfully develop from the comfort of your own armchair (or hammock if you prefer), spending as much, or as little, time as you want as you develop the knowledge and experience to extract cash from the markets.

The more enthusiastic among you may well be spending a lot more time and, as long as you follow the rules, this will be time well spent.

But, **discipline is more important than time**. Better to spend a little time and be disciplined when it comes to the market than to spend lots of time and lose that all-important discipline.

Section 5 –
Good Habits and
Bad Habits

IN THIS SECTION WE ARE GOING TO LOOK AT MANY OF THE PROBLEMS faced by traders and then look at what can be done to change the unsuccessful bad habits to successful good habits.

To a very large extent the following issues are all symptoms of one key mistake. That mistake is not to treat trading as a business. Or, to put this another way, not to think like a professional trader.

If you want to trade professionally you need to make sure you pay attention to the issues below.

TIMES HAVE CHANGED ...

If you think you have problems now, consider what faced me when I started back in the 1980s:

- No internet

- No smartphones

- Barely any computers

- No charting software, other than services like Reuters and Bloomberg at thousands per month

- Minimum trading size around £25 per point for futures and £10 per point for options with generally higher commissions

- Very few books available

- Very few UK trading advisory services (until I started *The Technical Trader* in 1989!)

Back then I used to prepare my charts by hand and, once I discovered the RSI, I used to work it out on a calculator (I forget the time span, maybe five-hour).

Matters started to improve when I bought Market Eye in 1987. Market Eye was a stand-alone price service, a bit like a small TV. I followed this with my first computer, an Apricot, in 1989. Together with programmer Peter Maher I developed Technical Trader charting software around the same time, so I started to get computerised. This process has continued to this very day; now I can get charts, via IG Index, on my smartphone and iPad, plus I can use my computer virtually anywhere, either with free Wi-Fi or mobile broadband.

Things have changed a lot in 25 years!

In fact at this point in the 21st century the markets are accessible for free to anyone who wants them pretty much 24/7 and companies are falling over each other to provide services to let you trade them.

All of this makes trading far, far easier; but in other ways it has got harder and more competitive. There are now far more traders than there were before and all these traders have many more tools and techniques than were previously available.

... BUT SOME THINGS REMAIN THE SAME

However all of this actually changes very little as far as winning and losing is concerned. The basic fact is still the same with 90% of traders losing and 5% winning and another 5% who are close but just spin their wheels as they do little more than break-even.

I am told that spread betting clients have an average account size of around £1500, although starting size will tend to be lower, and 90% of that starting money is lost in the first three to six months – so the big winners are the spread betting companies themselves – albeit they have to cover all that marketing expenditure plus opening offers. Make no mistake the losers pay for all this stuff!

Have you heard of the 90/90/90 rule?

Brokers and the spread betting companies talk about it a lot (but not to clients!). It says that 90% of clients will lose 90% of their capital in 90 days!

That will not change, for reasons I explain below. The purpose of this book is to put you in the winning 5%.

THE BENEFITS OF BEING IN THE 5%

The winning 5% is a great place to be, as I know from personal experience. Here are some of the key advantages of making the trading business work for you:

- You can work from anywhere you want. I have traded from tropical beaches, ski resorts and even, sometimes, from home.

- You can work when you want, or not work when you want.

- You have no clients or customers to worry about.

- Once you win the sky is the limit and the only limitation is your own psychology.

- You choose how much time to spend on your business.

- You are the boss.

All this good stuff only comes if you can rise above the one basic disadvantage you suffer and this is …

Your own psychology.

It is as simple, and as difficult, as that!

There are secondary issues too and some of these are set out below.

19 PROBLEMS

Why aren't you making as much money in the markets as you might?

For many people the reasons will include some of:

1. I have no clear system or methodology

2. I trade on impulse

3. I do not turn up for work consistently

4. I do not understand how markets work

5. I do not treat trading as a business

6. I have a clear system but I don't follow it

7. I keep missing all the best trades

8. I often lose far more than I mean to

9. I find I keep taking small profits and miss the big bonanza just around the corner

10. I trade emotionally

11. I follow a tipster but only occasionally

12. I have not taken the time to understand how markets work

13. I have never had any training and have no real idea what I am doing

14. I know I need a mentor but have made no effort to find one

15. I'm a born loser and don't know why I bother

16. I find it very difficult to trade in size but realise unless I do so I will never make enough money

17. I do not use Money Management effectively

18. I trade far more than I should

19. I'm just not worthy of this wealth and success and don't deserve it

These problems are all just symptoms of an underlying issue, which is not thinking and behaving like a professional trader.

Let's look at each of these in turn. I have included case studies of traders I have worked with to illustrate the respective problems.

Problem 1: I have no clear system or methodology

This often comes up as many new traders don't even know what a system or methodology is! They simply like the idea of trading and want to give it a go; this simple impulse is why 90% of them lose most of their cash within three months.

So what is a system or methodology?

It is a collection of rules which dictate when you take trades, the risk you allow and when you take profits. A system is a fairly rigid set of rules and may in fact be 100% mechanical, meaning that on any one day the system will tell you precisely what to do. A methodology is less rigid but still encompasses the way you trade. One of the key points here is that the system or methodology defines your focus, meaning the factors that you pay attention to. It is much easier to become an expert on a few factors than the entire market.

We have, of course, already looked at systems, methodology and focus earlier in this book.

Most people do not bother to learn anything about markets, do not go on any courses, and do not read any books.

In fact they spend less time preparing to enter one of the most competitive arenas on this planet than they would if they were going to play tennis, bridge, or bowls at the local club. So it is no surprise that most of them get cleaned out pretty quickly.

Actually this is good news, at least to an extent.

It is good news because *you* are not in that category because you are reading this book! Plus the money these guys are losing is money you can pick up by using better strategies allied with some trading discipline.

Damn, I mentioned the 'D' word!

A number of you will now have gone into panic mode realising that if discipline is involved, that means some effort will be involved and effort = hard work!

Yes, I'm afraid it's true; but better to find out now than realise only after you have lost a lot of cash.

However, let me ease your panic by adjusting that formula to 'disciplined effort = smart work'. But it most definitely involves some work.

If you don't want to make the necessary effort the best thing to do is close the account, take out the cash and forget about trading.

Better to do that now and avoid all the angst!

In my view a clear system/methodology is essential to success in the markets. Such a system may simply be viewed as a method to extract cash from the market. It will involve one or a number of techniques which you use in your trading and these may involve fundamental or technical analysis.

The range of possible techniques is pretty unlimited and can involve: the days of the week, months of the year, animals at the zoo, tea leaves, dartboards, the stars, shoeshine boys or taxi drivers, to name but a few – I am quite serious!

These various techniques may be applied in a totally mechanical fashion so your system is precise and can be back-tested (depending on the techniques involved) or it may be more flexible.

The key test is, does it work? Does it generate profit?

Having said all of this, there are a small number of gifted individuals who understand trading at a very basic level and win whatever – if you are one of those you are in a fortunate position. If not, you need a clear system/methodology.

Case study

Client A's problem was that he had made money consistently working on the floor of an exchange but found he could not duplicate his success working at home from a computer screen.

We worked together to carefully analyse the issue. It transpired that he had developed two primary systems whilst working on the floor, one to do with noise levels (which he found helpful in determining whether a break was true or false) and the other to do with the action of key traders on the floor. Neither system was now available; so we developed a new approach, playing to his strengths, which worked well.

Solution

This one is a doddle on one level – see the first four sections of this book. Elsewhere, I look at system testing and design in my book *Binary Trading*.

Problem 2: I trade on impulse

This problem goes hand in hand with the one before. If you have no system or methodology what else can you do but trade on impulse?

The problem with doing so is that you are, in effect, trading randomly and this is not effective in an environment with transactional costs. Even if you did achieve a situation where the trading results broke even, the costs involved would bring you down.

It is in the nature of trading and human psychology that we tend to take our profits too early, as we are used to grabbing the good stuff quickly, but we then let losses run, as we seek to avoid them. This psychological bias, in both cases based on the fear of losing something of value, is a major handicap in trying to make money out of markets but is eliminated when we use a clear and well-thought-out strategy.

A solution may seem to be to follow someone else's tips, but I have yet to meet the man (or woman) who does this consistently as people always miss trades for one reason or another and once you do this you are in a random process which is very similar to impulsive trading. Bear in mind the 80/20 rule – 80% of your profits will come from 20% of your trades and if you cherry-pick the trades, sod's law will come into play and you will miss some, maybe all, of the key 20% trades.

There are other reasons why you may miss the key 20%; two of the most common are:

1. They are often the most difficult trades to get on board, either because the action is fast or because it is completely at odds with the prevailing market psychology.

2. Even if you do get on board most traders fail to make the most of any move – this is, in fact, the most deadly of the trading sins and if you cannot overcome this you will *never* make good money in the markets.

A somewhat random process to following tips takes us back to the same parameters as impulsive trading with the same negative expectancy.

Impulsive trading tends to work out as being less successful even than random trading. Random trading will not work because it is liable to lead to a 50/50 result over time and this is useless when you factor in transaction costs. Impulsive trading is worse as it also leaves you open to market psychology, which will tend to lead you to do the wrong thing at the wrong time.

Case study

Trader B was having erratic results. She thought that her trading was based on sound principles but, once we had analysed what she was actually doing, it transpired that it had more to do with how she was feeling and her emotions than anything else. In this case her principles were sound, she was just not trading them correctly.

The solution here came in two parts. First we made her approach more mechanical so she could see more clearly when she was not following the trades correctly. Secondly we put in place a short checklist so she could gauge whether her emotions might get in the way.

Solution

At least you know what you should be doing, but it comes down to your trading psychology to make sure you do it. You may have been trading on impulse either because you had no system or because you did not know you needed one – now you do, so that will help.

However, we are going to the root of our humanity with this one. Some people are simply impulsive by nature and, if that's you, you will need to do one of two things:

1. Train yourself to act impulsively in line with your trading approach. This is quite possible but you may need to develop a system very closely aligned to your nature. Even impulsive behaviour is governed by our habits so you would need to make your system a good habit of yours.

2. Instil yourself with tougher discipline, but this may be an uphill battle for an impulsive trader. We are trying to find the easiest paths here, not the most difficult.

Problem 3: I do not turn up for work consistently

This is a big issue for traders generally and it is one that any trader with aspirations to go professional has to deal with. We all turn up for work in the 'real' world and we need to do exactly the same when we are trading.

Your working hours will be determined by your Focus and your System/Methodology. Referring again to *ZeitGap*, you need to be on station when the DAX opens at 08h00 – I would suggest starting earlier so that you are fully prepared for the opening, say 07h45. If you do not do so then you may well miss that day's trade and you will be creating losing habits which you will later find hard to correct.

You are either in the business of trading in which case you need to treat it seriously or you are not, in which case you are involved in what may become a very expensive hobby.

Solution

This is a major issue with many traders and the solution comes in one or two distinct forms:

1. **Buy an alarm clock!**

2. If this is not your business then suit yourself (but do not expect too much); if it is your business **decide now to make it work and turn up for work**!

Problem 4: I do not understand how markets work

The majority think financial markets are all about the news. As usual the majority have got it wrong!

But as with all great myths there is an element of truth in it. News comes out and the market jerks around as if something has happened, but this is only a small part of the story. The actual determinant of market action is buying and selling. This ultimately governs price, so if we want to understand markets we need to focus on this factor. Here are a few of the factors affecting buying and selling:

1. availability of cash,

2. existing positions,

3. the economy,

4. news flow, and

5. sentiment (i.e. human psychology).

The market is many things but I think the best description is: a *maelstrom of human psychology*. Although this describes the experience, the market is also a machine governed by fairly strict rules and as we examine the factors that affect buying and selling these rules will become clear.

Let's look more closely at these five factors.

1. Availability of cash

The first factor is how much cash investors at large have to invest. In good times, as in the run-up to 1999 and 2007, investors had plenty of cash and a good slab of that made it into the market, propelling prices higher. All pretty clear and simple. QE (quantitative easing, a financial experiment started in 2009) has had a similar effect.

2. Existing positions

This factor is vital. If an individual investor already has a substantial holding in a particular stock, let's take Apple as an example, then he is less likely to buy more, especially if that stock increases in price and starts to form a disproportionately large part of the portfolio.

But it is more fundamental than that; the fact is:

Every time somebody buys a stock the market gets weaker!

Now this is a fairly controversial statement. It is contrary to the mass perception and is also totally counter-intuitive.

But any auction process does this. As price goes up it makes it more expensive to buy, thus reducing the number of buyers. At the same time it becomes more attractive to sell.

Price is a function of supply and demand. Rising prices serve to increase supply, as more sellers come in, and reduce demand as buyers withdraw. This is what we might call Markets 101.

There are other forces at work too. A rising market triggers greed and some buyers are compelled to join in at ever more idiotic prices because of that emotional factor, but these people are not serious market participants and become what is termed *weak holders* who will quickly jump ship when the market turns against them. In fact the presence of such buyers is one factor that determines that we are in a bubble. As history has shown, such bubbles can last much longer than might be expected.

Let's say an investor holds no shares in Apple Inc. and he has the potential to buy the stock. As the stock price increases it exerts a hypnotic influence on investors to buy the stock, encouraged by the feedback from other investors they talk to saying how much money they are making. So whilst the investor holds no stock in Apple he can still be viewed as a potential positive for the stock because he *may* buy it.

But consider what happens when he has bought it. Firstly that potential positive is no more but, more importantly, the potential positive has reversed into a potential negative because now *he may sell the stock.*

So price may have increased as that investor, and possibly others, bought the stock, but the market has weakened because all those buyers who had the potential to buy now have the potential to sell.

Surely, I hear you say, as one person buys the stock someone else is selling it? In fact this is not always the case as the company itself may issue new stock. Even where there is a transaction between a buyer and a seller, we can still see a difference because in a rising market the buyer will likely have bought the stock at a higher price. Those who buy at higher prices will tend to be weaker holders more prone to get out more quickly. This may be particularly true at major peaks where prices may subsequently be described as idiotic.

Now take this to its logical conclusion.

The stock continues to rally and as it does so the hypnotic effect on the minds of investors becomes irresistible and more and more investors buy the stock. Usually at this point there is not a cloud in the sky, adding to the euphoria and greed that pushes investors to buy at silly prices – they may not seem silly at the time but looked at in the cold light of day, away from all this emotion, that is exactly what they are.

So the buying continues and the positive potential, measured by those who do not own the stock but *may* buy, dwindles away (such buyers either not being interested at the prices available or having already bought unable to resist the hypnotic allure of the market) to be replaced by the negative potential, measured by those who hold the stock but *may* sell.

Plus a lot of these are now weak holders: meaning they bought at silly prices and are very vulnerable to a pullback. It does not take that many sellers to push a market down substantially, for example I understand less than 10% of stocks were sold during the 1987 crash!

To make an additional point, take the investor who sold Apple at, say, $200 on the way up. I would say that he or she is very unlikely to be a buyer at $500 or above. OK, very few investors act rationally as they are too hyped up with emotion, and in fact it is the investors who overcome this emotion who make all the money.

If an investor is acting rationally when he sold at $200 there is no way he would buy at $500, unless something fairly major had changed and this is unlikely. But if he had been acting emotionally, which is more likely, it is also unlikely he would buy at the higher price as it would mean admitting he had been wrong to sell at the lower price and people hate to do that!

So a point is reached where the negative potential becomes overwhelming and the stock starts to fall. Very often there is no news of import to justify this but market pundits hate that and start to scratch their heads and play the game I call 'sticking the news tail on the market donkey'. The game that is played blindfold, which aptly describes their blinkered view of how the market works.

So, even though the fall happens because 'everyone' has bought, the man/woman in the street listens to the experts who spout nonsense based on some obscure news item these experts think has caused the change!

It is my view that the factors stated above are the major determinants in the *timing* of the major moves in stocks – the main determinants in bull *and* bear markets!

3. The economy

Of course the economy also has a large effect as it determines how much cash is in the system and thus how much investors have to invest.

What of government policy?

This is not completely irrelevant but generally the less a government does, the better – a factor I believe applies to pretty much every area in which the government gets involved, other than its primary duties such as public order and defence.

A free market which is properly self-regulated wins hands down on every occasion and the price mechanism itself looks after most problem areas; by contrast governments can put many spanners in the works.

For example a government may decide to ban short selling because they feel stocks are going too low. Such action is most often followed by sharp falls where the market is said to have no bottom. The logic is clear, as follows.

I said above that every time an investor buys stock it weakens the market because he has the potential to sell. The reverse holds true when a short seller comes along and such action strengthens the market (whilst very possibly driving price lower) because they have the potential to buy. In fact these guys provide a floor, they provide a bottom, because as price goes lower they will start buying.

It is when you ban short selling that the market truly has no bottom and this is a clear case of fear (the fear of falling markets) creating the very thing that is feared – a common occurrence which is why we should never be swayed by fear.

In fact when it comes to the economy the government is really in the position of a surfer. They do their best to look good surfing the waves but have as little control over the waves of the economy as a surfer does over the waves of the sea.

They can most certainly screw things up, but business is best left to businessmen who will make the most of the opportunities. Certainly the worst excesses of such businessmen need to be controlled and that is a proper function of government – but it always goes far too far, bowing to various pressure groups and creating mess and muddle in the process.

This trend of too much government is why we in the West are now in such a non-competitive situation as compared to the new economies in the East that are not burdened by excess government, excess welfare, and excess taxes.

If we study history it is when government gets too big that empires decline and, finally, fall. The British Empire peaked in the 19th century and I would say the US is now in the peaking process. The mantle will undoubtedly pass to the East.

(I am writing this section in Bangkok and I have no doubt this will be one of the leading cities in the world within the next 10 or 20 years – in fact if you want to invest in property you should certainly consider Bangkok as one possibility. Right now, in 2015, there is some political risk with an ageing monarch, but I cannot see anything really halting growth in this area.)

This leaves two final factors to consider.

4. News flow

Many consider news flow the prime determinant of market action. I consider it almost entirely irrelevant most of the time.

As I said at the beginning of this section, news does affect short-term action as traders react to the latest newsflash, but this means nothing really. News is mainly concerned with the economy and a single issue of a particular economic indicator in itself is rarely critical, especially when fudged by various government agencies and seasonally adjusted, etc. What is important is the trend of such indicators over time, but a single release does not show that.

Certainly there are significant news items, such as interest rate hikes, fiscal cliffs, bankruptcy or an earthquake, but, important as these are, they do not usually change trends, although they may mark the beginning or end of such.

From the trading standpoint although news may not be important in the grander scheme of things it can be critically important when it comes to shorter-term trading – in fact I have developed trading systems based entirely on news items (included in my books *Binary Trading* and *Tunnel Trading*). I should mention that these systems pay no heed to the content of the news itself, merely the possible market reaction.

One particular aspect of news is that it can lead to sharp knee-jerk action and this can all too easily knock out trading positions if stop losses are in place close to market action and, in some cases, not so close. This is one good reason why a trader needs to know when news comes out even if he/she has little interest in what the news might actually be (which is my basic position).

5. Sentiment (human psychology)

Whilst news flow may be the least significant of our factors, human psychology is definitely the most important. If you agree that the markets are a maelstrom of human psychology, and I believe this is indisputable, then clearly human psychology is what it is all about. Remember you cannot do anything without engaging your psychology.

Information comes into our brains (our three brains – see *The Way to Trade*) and it gets processed. This can then result in action being either impulsive, emotional or thoughtful depending on which brain is dominant, stimulated and/or effective at that time.

In general the process goes like this, and in this order:

1. something happens in your environment and your **survival brain** checks to see if there is imminent danger to you,

2. your **emotional brain** then decides which emotional state is needed to handle this event (i.e. fear, anger, happiness), and

3. if there is no danger, and your emotions are in check, you may have time to **think logically** about what is happening and make a logical decision about how to behave in relation to the event.

However, if either (1) or (2) shift you into survival mode, don't expect (3) to be available until the perceived threat has been dealt with or your self-control allows you to reduce the influence of your survival mechanism.

With market action, 99.9% is dictated by this process and so human psychology holds sway. But there are also algorithms at work (aka trading robots), which are created by human psychology but are then let loose to work on their own within preset limits. The Flash Crash in May 2010 is an example of their work. It is interesting, and rather alarming, that these emotionless robots seem capable of producing more erratic action than massed humanity at its least rational.

I hope this brief look at what markets are gives you some insight into what you are dealing with. It is certainly fascinating and I could write a lot more just on this single aspect. For example, I have only briefly mentioned the auction process above, which some (including me) see as a fundamental aspect of the market.

Solution

We have covered various aspects of this so you should now be a lot further forwards. Please be aware we will never understand markets fully, but you now know a lot more.

The key thing is to develop a positive trading state so your mind and body are in the best condition for the trading environment.

Problem 5: I do not treat trading as a business

It is not up to me to tell you how to live your life and there is absolutely nothing wrong with coming into the market with a view to enjoying your trading or to simply make life more entertaining and interesting. *But* if you want to succeed then hard work is required and many people see this as incompatible with having fun.

What does 'trading as a business' mean?

As with any business it means most of the following:

- Testing out the idea at low/zero risk. Trading the methodology either on paper or via a dummy account.

- Once you have found an edge you start to trade for real but with low sums as there are three key techniques required for trading success:

  1. Your system/methodology

  2. Money Management

  3. Your trading psychology

- You properly develop your Money Management systems which ensure that you never risk too much on any one trade and that you maximise returns by trading at appropriate levels.

- You must watch your revenue and also, of course, your costs – just like any other good businessman.

- As profits start to roll in you reinvest in your business (and yourself) by doing further research and by expanding your trading size – if you don't do this you will never reap the kind of rewards you may want. One aspect that may need to be considered is mental and psychological blocks which may stand in the way of your success.

- Good businessmen also look to expand their businesses on top of the original functions. This makes a lot of sense and once you are a successful trader a wealth of opportunity presents itself. Here are a few of the factors you might consider:

  1. Taking on new traders to explore new markets and new techniques (an area that is of interest to me right now)

  2. Fund management

  3. Writing books – there is great demand for books by those who are successful

4. Seminars, courses and DVDs

5. Market services

6. Market systems

7. Consultancy/mentorship

8. Advising other traders, hedge funds, etc.

None of this is obligatory but these are further options you might consider.

Reading this book is a start but this goes a lot deeper. Most people have been conditioned to behave themselves, not just socially (which is a very good thing), but in the sense that they do not want to disrupt the status quo and change things. But change is essential if you want to transform your life. You need to take control and this can be a huge, life-changing step for many people.

Solution

If you do not treat trading as a business you will not make money. Clearly this is not compulsory and I know traders who trade for fun, at a price, and those who just want to keep busy in their retirement, which makes a lot of sense as you keep younger if you keep active.

So this is a choice, just like wealth is a choice – it is up to you to make the choice you wish!

Having made the choice you need to stay focused and persevere. Everything in life is a choice, make no mistake about that, but making the choice alone is, sadly, not going to do it. There is hard work involved, usually lots of it, and setbacks along the way. Every setback, every failure, takes you forward as you learn – so increase your failures and you automatically increase your rate of progress.

Whilst doing this, make sure you are making money, as you need money to keep going. There is absolutely no point in unnecessarily wiping yourself out. There again this can be the biggest learning experience of all, one I have been through, as have many leading entrepreneurs.

So everything in life is a choice and there are sacrifices to be made to reach your goals.

Of course your choice may be to do nothing, to simply coast along and see what comes up. This is what the 90% do and they rarely get anywhere. Many don't even know they are making this choice and they may prefer not to know, rather than know and then fail.

Every now and then one of this multitude gets lucky and lands a major win on the lottery or some such, keeping hope eternal for the rest – but the odds of this happening are akin to getting run over by a bus.

90% are always going to struggle, while 5% have made it. But what of the remaining 5%? Well this group has two components. One component is those who have chosen to be wealthy but are still in the process. The other component is those who have made the choice but are floundering on the way. Some of these will give up and slip back into the 90%.

It is the giving up which is the defining moment; once you do that the game is over.

Problem 6: I have a clear system but I don't follow it

This is a biggie.

You put in the work and either buy or build a system; you may even do a bit of both, buying a system then modifying it to suit you. You carefully test it out and it works! Yippee, you are well on the road to success.

But then, and many of you reading this may not be able to believe this, you simply don't follow it.

I've been through this myself. It is all too easy to second-guess any system, to avoid trades you don't like for one reason or another, to still trade emotionally, and to take other non-system trades you do like.

The net result of all this is we don't really have a system, at least not one we use, and so we are pretty much back to square one – impulsive trading!

The solution lies partially in discipline and partially in habit forming. You need to be strict with yourself, trade the system and make it a winning habit.

Of course it can be at just the time you take this decision, having missed a great string of winners, that the markets serve you a googly and you end up with four losses in a row! But you need to persevere. All systems have a run like this and if you have put in the groundwork you *know* it works over time.

The big issue with any trading is that losses arise regularly. We all like to think we can be disciplined but the reality is often very different from this especially if the market has 'punished' us a few times recently. In this context the cost of trading – the spread or a broker's commissions – make it even more painful. You might set up your system to give you equal profits and losses, only to realise belatedly that each profit is reduced by the spread and every loss is enhanced by it. Brokers' commissions have the same effect. Clearly this needs to be taken into account when you research your trading system in the first place.

There are only two options here. Either you follow the system or you go back to the drawing board and research again. A third option may appear to be to use the system with some discretion, but this also needs research to test out the ideas so it is really just option two disguised.

I should add that systems do not need to be 100% mechanical; you can allow yourself as much discretion as you need. The key is that the system gives you an edge and that you have the discipline to follow it.

Solution

This can also be a choice or we may be back with impulsive or emotional behaviour, in which case my earlier comments apply.

Problem 7: I keep missing all the best trades

I touched on this above, but there is bound to be some repetition in these various categories. My intention is to cover all of the main reasons why your trading may not live up to expectations and this is the biggest problem I encounter with otherwise fairly proficient traders.

You may have a good system, solid Money Management and solid trading psychology, but if you miss the best trades you are never going to make much money. It is like working all month and then not bothering to pick up your salary cheque at the end!

Let's look at why the best trades may be eluding you:

1. The **signals can be fast** – traders talk about the train leaving the station with as few passengers on board as possible. If you are not poised and ready when the trade signal is given you may be faced with greater risk than you like and simply not take the trade. But you cannot afford to miss these trades. So you need to be ready and you need to deal with the higher risk; if that is the only alternative then you could reduce position size.

2. The system signals can be **against the prevailing mass psychology** (i.e. buying in a major bear market, or selling when everybody else is saying how wonderful everything is). A trader needs to ignore the masses, who are *always* wrong at major turning points! Of course, you are a human being too and so you are part of this mass psychology and it can be difficult to take trades like this. But very often these are the best trades; everyone is positioned the wrong way so all those traders bailing out will make the trade go a lot further than usual.

3. **Sod's law** also applies: the law that states if you do the wrong thing it will undoubtedly be at the wrong time, and if you finally do the right thing it also will undoubtedly be at the wrong time. So if something comes up and you miss a trade it is likely to be a good one. This merely underlines how seriously you need to treat your trading. Sod's law also states if you start to do something or stop doing something both of these are also likely to be at the wrong time.

Case study

This is another issue I come across again and again and so I am combining my advice to each trader in this summary. In the case of 1 above it is all about being prepared (and maybe being sure to set that alarm clock). Point 2 is a more pressing problem and if you find it hard to go against the herd, which can be a big survival issue, then you may need some help. There is no escape from 3 I'm afraid, but solid preparation will only help (even if you do it at the wrong time!).

Solution

This is a major problem and you will never make it if you struggle with this. There are valid, practical reasons why this can happen but you have to overcome them.

Again, it comes down to choice.

One aspect is designing your trading approach around your lifestyle. There is no point trying to use a system that trades at 08h00 if you are always doing something else at that time. For example, *ZeitGap* usually trades at this time which is one reason why I have developed a similar system on the NASDAQ as this trades in the afternoon (in the UK – obviously trading times will be different depending on where you are based).

But even though you may have designed your system to suit your lifestyle there will still be times when it will be all too easy to be doing something else when trading time comes around.

Now with a system like *ZeitGap* you will know when there is only a small profit on offer and it is then not so important, but you cannot afford to miss the big profit opportunities. Other systems are not so accommodating, especially those designed to catch the major trends, or for example a system trading triangles where very big moves and profits can and will be at stake.

Problem 8: I often lose far more than I mean to

This is more of a novice mistake, but it can also creep up on experienced traders as they try out different approaches to risk control.

The classic novice mistake is to lose so much that one trade wipes you out; that is when many learn they need risk control in the first place. Many traders go through this experience; I did myself back in the 1980s. Certainly it is best avoided, but as learning experiences go it is very effective.

Similarly many top entrepreneurs have, at some point in their earlier careers, been made bankrupt or come very close. If you google 'well-known bankruptcies' you may be surprised at what you find.

All trading is a trade-off between your profits and your losses. You cannot afford to lose more than you plan to win on a regular basis – it is like selling your widget for $1 and then finding out it cost you $2! A business doing that would not last long and so it is with trading.

Case study

This can be a complex issue as the reasons for such behaviour can run deep. For example, Trader A was a very keen sportsman and his will to win, the determination *not* to lose, was causing this problem with his trading.

This trader had built up his determination to win partly by doing everything he could not to lose. But in the markets it is much better to lose a small sum, as per your trading plan, than to battle away and then lose a much bigger sum. In this case Trader A was achieving his goal of not giving up by adding to losing positions. Sometimes this would work, but when it did not he would face unacceptable losses.

Solution

Any good business will keep a tight control on costs. The losses you make are a major cost against your revenue – so they need to be controlled.

OK, occasionally bad things happen, and you may end up with a lot more slippage than you would normally expect or circumstances conspire against you, *but* you need to learn from these occasions.

Here are a few of the situations which you must not let happen:

- Forgetting to, or deciding not to, place a stop.

- Removing your stop as the market nears it.

- Overtrading – in this case meaning trading in too big a size for your pot.

- Getting carried away because you see a certainty – there ain't no such thing.

- Adding to losing positions, unless it is part of a careful risk-controlled strategy.

None of these are acceptable, except perhaps in the first case above, but only if your risk control system does not use stops. This is completely valid (see *The Way to Trade*) and is simply another way of trading. Generally you will be trading in much smaller size, in relation to your pot, but taking stops out of the equation makes everything far more straightforward.

We have already discussed the difficulty in coming back from a big loss so you simply cannot afford to make losses bigger than you planned to.

Problem 9: I find I keep taking small profits and miss the big bonanza just around the corner

This is one of the matters I discussed when looking at why it can be hard to catch (and stay with) the best trades. In the next section we will be looking at this in detail.

I hear this so often as traders battered by the market have become fearful of trading. They are so busy trying to keep risk to the bare minimum that they grab any profit going, however small it may be.

Solution

We have already covered this under missing the best trades.

Let's assume you do get on board *all* of your trades. It is so easy to find yourself taking small profits and you will make no progress if you do not capture the big profits. In fact it can be a very instinctive action that easily becomes a habit.

I've done it myself. In fact, I have done all this stuff – don't for one minute think I am writing this from some imagined position of superiority. I very much practise what I preach and the only reason I have got where I am today is because I have failed and failed again.

Even now I sometimes take those small profits; sometimes I do this before I realise what is going on. As I said, this can be an instinctive reaction and instincts and emotions work far faster than thought.

But in these cases I have trained myself to only take partial profits – leaving part of the trade open for further gains – and I am quick to use *Xtreme Stop* (see Appendix 1 for more information) to ensure I am repositioned if I got it wrong.

Problem 10: I trade emotionally

In my view this is the big bugbear faced by us humans when it comes to trading. Fundamentally we live our lives in an emotional world; that is where we feel, where we are happy or sad. Our brains may have three channels and the thoughtful and instinctive channels are dominant in many of us, but we feel our results via our emotions.

In addition many of us are used to getting what we want and getting it now – this is an emotional frame of mind and when translated into market action becomes:

"I want to trade and I want to trade NOW!"

This type of impatience can lead you to impulsive trading and to ignoring your system.

You may not notice this as it tends to happen subconsciously or at least beyond your awareness level. You can change this if you focus carefully on what you do and why you do it – in fact this sort of personal analysis can be invaluable.

The point I am making is that we may spend weeks and months developing our systems and testing them out and then, on the day, we may take a number of random trades because of our emotions – of which impatience is but one. At the first sensation of impatience take remedial action to curb it before it drives you to act against your best interests.

My comments above on trading on impulse are also relevant here.

Solution

We have touched on this already.

I will add one factor I covered in *The Way to Trade* which is that it is sometimes hard to see our wayward emotions and this is where a system can be vital. At the theatre, stagehands wear black so they cannot be seen against a black background and this is akin to trading without a system; it is all black and we cannot see how our minds work. Introduce a system that tells you what you should be doing and suddenly those stagehands are in a bright spotlight and they can be easily seen.

For example, your system says do X but you do Y. Aha, now you know something is afoot and it is pretty much bound to be due to instincts and emotions. These instincts and emotions can seem pesky in your trading, and indeed they are often counterproductive in this arena, but for many areas of life they are invaluable and they are one of the reasons humans thrive on earth.

Once you know what is going on it is much easier to deal with and this is one of the reasons why I think trading a system is a vital stage in the progress of any trader. I have not changed from this view in over two decades!

Problem 11: I follow a tipster but only occasionally

Tipsters come in all shapes and sizes; some are great, some are average, and some are downright awful! Even if you subscribe to the best tipster in the world he will still have losing trades and his success will be based on probability and statistics. By this I mean that a good tipster will have an edge but that edge will be produced randomly over the various trades thus producing results which may appear inconsistent.

If you do not take all of the trades, or stay with them as recommended, you are back to trading randomly. You may be missing the best trades and you only need to miss one or two of them to destroy the whole concept.

Of course you may use a tipster (aka market analyst or guru) to add to your trading ideas and this is a different kettle of fish.

I have met a few traders who do well from following other traders but usually it is the ideas that prove useful rather than the actual trades. The important thing is to build up a methodology that you can use independently.

Solution

This comes back to taking all the trades and staying with them (i.e. no bailing out with small profits).

It can be more difficult to stay with trades somebody else gives you as you may not fully understand the rationale of each trade. This is why I always explain the basis of any recommendation in my own trading service.

Problem 12: I have not taken the time to understand how markets work

Another big reason why many traders get cleaned out in the first few months. This is another degree of idiocy beyond "I do not understand how markets work", as in that category we might assume that the individual has at least made some effort to understand but has swallowed a load of pap in the process.

No one reading this book can be said to fall into this category as you are now taking the time, whatever you may have done in the past, so feel free to pat yourself on the back!

Case study

None, as I never get to meet these people.

Solution

I would hope you now know a lot more than you did when you started this book.

However we have really only scratched the surface and this is a matter requiring further research. Of course every trade you do is research of sorts. And a full understanding of the market is simply not possible. Just think of all the possible information that is available, all the shares, indices and other instruments, all the constantly changing prices and news items, all the market participants and their varying views and actions.

We are forced to choose our focus and that focus says a lot about the way we will trade. In my view the ultimate focus is our trading system.

Incidentally, focus is also a key part of life itself and allied with depth pretty much defines our lives. Depth in this context relates to how deeply we focus on particular areas of our lives, trading being the focus at this point.

Problem 13: I have never had any training and have no real idea what I am doing

This is similar to the previous category, although training is a degree higher than simply acquiring a basic understanding. In any other field of human endeavour we tend to get trained before we start doing something. We also learn loads of stuff by ourselves by observing others.

In the markets there is a vast array of training available but not all of it is useful. Due to the uncertain nature of future action it is all too simple to formulate an approach which can demonstrate superior performance in the past but with zero (or less) practical application for the future. There are also many rogues very happy to offer expensive training programmes that won't help you at all and as such you need to be careful.

Some traders look down on training and seminars. Some finally overcome this but fail to shrug off the negativity, which is not helpful. Those who are determined use every opportunity to learn and they finally get somewhere. Too many either never start or fall by the wayside.

Solution

Reading a book is a good start down this road. A good book is worth many, many times the cost of entry.

Trading the right way is also training, but trading emotionally can be a disaster with bad habits forming by the dozen.

Meeting up with other traders at seminars and conferences can also be extremely useful. You will find that the people who want to make progress do not think twice about laying out some cash for these events.

I used to be surprised when very successful people signed up for seminars. *Surely they knew it all already?* I then realised that this was how they got to be so successful in the first place.

Of course, if you frequent trading bulletin boards (BBs), you will hear how all these events are rip-offs and every market service is a scam. But the guys who frequent the BBs are going nowhere and will still be writing the same sad stuff years from now.

So if you want to be successful I would suggest doing what the successful do: they are very happy, maybe even desperate, to spend cash to make fast progress. These guys use the material, work with it, and make progress.

The key point is you need to believe that you are worth the investment in yourself.

Problem 14: I know I need a mentor but have made no effort to find one

Mentorship is a degree above training. The key aspect with a mentor is not that they may know how to do what you want to do, but that they have *done* it! Once you have done something, you know with absolute certainty that it can be done and that is what you want the mentor to pass to you – certainty is *very* valuable.

Personally I only realised this a few years ago, rather late in the process. I was reading an interview with Richard Branson who said, that at the age of 15, he realised he needed a mentor and I suspect this is one of the key reasons why he has achieved so much in his life.

I appreciate that mentors are not that easy to find but this can be a step that really speeds you along the road to success.

Solution

This is more complex than mere training; mentorship involves a close personal relationship. If you can find someone you know and like who has the expertise and has done what you aspire to then you are fortunate.

I believe this is one of the reasons why it is so important to have a peer group that supports what you want to achieve and not pour scorn on your aspirations. See *Think and Grow Rich* by Napoleon Hill (the book should have been called *Think, Do and Grow Rich*).

There are solutions to all challenges and if you are going to get where you want to be you have to learn the habit of finding those solutions.

Problem 15: I'm a born loser and don't know why I bother

This statement is just an excuse for sitting on your, possibly overlarge, behind and not getting out there and doing stuff.

Nobody is a born loser; it is a choice you make. However it is sad, but true, that 5% of us strive and get things done and 90% don't. The other 5% are undecided. This has always been the case and it is a factor that drives the self-help community to despair. A lot of the self-help experts genuinely want to help other people, just as I am writing this book to help traders. The fact that 95 people out of 100 derive little benefit is something they would love to change, and not just from the business standpoint. Certainly 100 satisfied customers out of 100 is great for business but we all get a lot more satisfaction by helping other people – I'm sure you all know that.

In fairness, the self-help experts do understand that 'losers' might actually have deep-rooted beliefs that are holding the person back and that these beliefs are often given to the person in childhood by unthinking parents and teachers. The common belief "I'm useless and good for nothing", which is often repeated to a child who simply doesn't do what an adult expects, can prevent that child from achieving in adult life – even though they may want to succeed.

Solution

You are not a born loser! You may think you are but that is just another example of human psychology.

I appreciate that it may be difficult to shake a belief like this which may be deeply held, in fact you may need help from someone like Les Meehan, who is a Success Performance Coach.

As an alternative my suggestion is practical. Just start doing stuff. Everything you do may either result in some form of failure, in which case you will learn something, or success, in which case you will be proving you are not a born loser.

Keep doing stuff until you are failing at least once every day. As you do this you will acquire skills and you will find your success rate steadily grows.

At the start of the process maybe you will mainly fail, but then you will start to succeed. Soon it will be 50/50 and shortly after that you will have trouble failing once a day as you will be too busy having multiple successes.

You just have to start!

This is not just a trading thing – it will work in any aspect of life you choose.

Problem 16: I find it very difficult to trade in size but realise unless I do so I will never make enough money

This problem is ultimately what trading is all about. In the markets size does matter!

It is certainly true that you do not want to be trading in size until you have dealt with all the issues in this section of the book. But once you have done so a failure to trade in size will doom you to never being able to buy the good stuff in life through your trading.

Let me define size.

Some clients I have trade at £500 per point. That is definitely size! But it is not a size you need to worry about until you are ready for it, and some may prefer to stick at lower levels.

Personally I have traded at the £500 level and above but these days I tend to stick to a maximum of around £50 per point.

Let's look at this from the aspect of how many points you may get out of the market in any month. Some traders have developed short-term strategies that may pull in a 100+ points per month, but these strategies often include very tight stops.

Size is not actually the major focus – it is risk you need to look at. If trading a £10,000 account then a risk level of 2% to 4% is recommended. On £10,000 that equates to a total risk of £200 to £400.

So your size depends on your stop, or where you would get out of the position. If you are going to risk 10 points then you can go in at £40 per point if you want to go for 4% (10 points at £40 per point = £400). But if your risk is 40 points then you can only trade at £10 per point.

Looking at a trade that is £500 per point with a 10 point stop, the total risk is thus £5000 (10 points at £500 per point = £5000) and this would meet the 4% rule if the account size was £125,000.

So bringing in 100 points per month is very different if you use a 10 point stop and can thus trade at £40 per point than if you use a 40 point stop reducing your size to £10 per point.

At £40 per point you would make £4000 per month, but at £10 per point you would be down to £1000 per month.

To put this another way, your profitability is determined by two main factors:

1. Account size

2. Your stop

Obviously it also depends on your trading skills and how the market decides to behave in that particular period – all systems take drawdowns.

Many of my clients are quite content with a profit of around £2000 per month in the early days, but it does depend on what you want – as I said, wealth is a choice!

Plus do not forget that trading is not an easy option and losses do occur.

Case study

Again I come across many traders who are not reaching their full potential because they cannot bump up size. There are many reasons for this and, often, they are right not to increase size because they have not reached the right trading stage due to one or more issues which I cover in this section.

From what I have learned working with clients, increasing trade size can be a challenge to:

- Self-confidence
- Confidence in the system being used
- Confidence in the advice received
- Fear of loss

For some people, the fear of loss increases rapidly as the trade size increases (understandably, as of course the potential loss is greater).

Solution

To an extent this is the message of the entire book. There is nothing wrong in trading at whatever size you wish but if you want your trading business to pay the bills and give you total financial freedom you have to trade at a size that will do that.

I have mentioned *wealth is a choice* a few times and I see this as a key message. It really is a choice, just like health and happiness are choices, and every day we are making decisions which either take us nearer or further away from what we really want. A lot of these decisions are habits, meaning they are decisions we have put onto a form of autopilot, but we can choose to become aware of these decisions and we can choose to change the way we live our lives.

I am not saying this is easy, I am just saying it is a choice.

We can choose to take action, we can choose to transform into what we want to be. We can choose to work with people who will help us. Or … we can choose not to.

Fairly simple really!

Problem 17: I do not use Money Management effectively

This is pretty much fatal and it can be a mercy if the end comes quickly!

There are two key points.

1. The first is that losses are going to occur and, in the simplest case, where you bet all your pot on every trade you just need that one loser and you are out for the count. OK, that is fairly obvious.

2. The second is a little more complicated and stems from the fact that, over time, strings of losses will come in. You need to be prepared for this (which is why I suggest risking 2% to 4% of your pot).

Case study

I have come across very few traders who take Money Management very seriously, but it is essential. Most traders are not sufficiently disciplined.

Solution

The rules discussed in this book are fairly basic. Mainly it can be summarised as do not risk too much on any one position (or linked positions).

There are gamblers who happily risk it all on one throw of the dice but I doubt any of those are reading this book! Obviously such a strategy is never going to work, unless you win on the first throw and then quit forever.

For the rest of you, the key point is risk only small portions of your capital on each trade. As you know the maximum risk should be 4%. That keeps you safe. More than that and you are liable to set yourself back months, maybe years.

Now there are more advanced techniques whereby you reduce your stakes as a string of losses comes in, maybe aggressively, and increase stakes as profits come in, but doing this depends on the parameters and profit/loss of your system. I have given some examples of the latter in Section Three.

Ultimately using Money Management effectively is part of your choice. If you don't use it you are choosing not to be wealthy.

Problem 18: I trade far more than I should

This is probably the major issue for many traders who are beyond the novice stage.

I work with many traders and this is a recurring issue. Forget emotional trading – the real problem occurs once a trade has been actioned, often correctly. If the trade is a loser many traders then seem bent on revenge, wanting to get back at the market and trading, often again and again, to break-even.

Often these *revenge trades* succeed, which is perhaps the worst that can happen and the habit can become well established. It is a losing habit, even if on occasion it wins. This is the essence of *random reinforcement* in the markets whereby the market is continually rewarding bad trading and punishing good trading.

Random reinforcement is one of the reasons learning to trade is tough.

Revenge trades are only part of the problem, as there can also be a tendency to trade some more even when the first trade is a winner. "I'm on a roll" the trader says to himself, or "I must reinvest some of my winnings" or it may be simply overconfidence caused by the euphoria of the win. An unfortunate cycle can be created where after every correct trade the trader finds himself trading again and again.

These extraneous and emotionally-driven trades often wipe out any profits that would have been made and they need to be eliminated.

Another part of the same issue is entering a valid position and then closing it for no good reason.

Many, many traders trade far too frequently and eliminate the profits they would have made if they had kept it simple.

Less is more!

Solution

This comes down to discipline, which in turn is about resisting emotional and instinctive trading impulses.

Problem 19: I'm just not worthy of this wealth and success and don't deserve it

We all deserve it, but we do need to learn to accept this. It is amazing how many ways we can self-sabotage ourselves; this is a very expensive way to live our lives. This problem is somewhat outside my area of expertise and I will hand you over to Les Meehan, who says:

> "The sense that we don't deserve things – e.g. success, wealth, happiness – is often related to our self-worth. The development of our self-worth is most often impacted by our early experiences when we may have been made to feel that what we do, say, or think has no value. This may manifest in traumatic ways, such as through some form of physical or mental bullying, or in more subtle ways such as having our opinions and ideas regularly rejected by our caregivers (parents, family) or people we hold as authority figures (teachers, friends). A classic example of the latter is seen in school reports. The famous 'could do better' found on many

school reports is probably the most insidious and regular form of self-worth erosion many young people experience. There has been research done with sales people that shows such comments on school reports have a strong negative impact on their earning potential and may contribute at an unconscious level to an early exit from a sales career.

"The first step to resolving the self-worth limitations and learning that you do in fact deserve everything that you create in your life is to be aware of such past experiences and to resolve the emotional trauma they have created and which is still deep within you."

Case study

Trader X was having issues with his relationship with money and consulted with Les. Here is his experience in his own words:

My experience has certainly been an interesting and surprising one. The journey into one's mind is not always a straightforward affair as I'm sure you know.

In my case, somehow my money matrix took a big dent helping family members after the storm in the Philippines in 2013 and left me feeling that money had no real worth. That and my feeling that money had to be earned on a fair wage for a fair day's work left me feeling uncomfortable about making lots of money without seemingly too much effort. All this came as a real surprise to me and explained my recent ambivalence over my trades, which makes for unhappy and unsettled trading.

The big lesson I have learned from this experience is that your mind can really be affected by external events in subtle ways you would least expect. This change then becomes part of your everyday living fabric without you realising it – very similar to a software virus on your computer. The only way to sort it out is with specialist help.

Through Les I've now learned how to use parts of my body as an effective trigger for instant recall of mood memories. This is sometimes known as Belief Tapping and Belief Location Reassignment in the brain. I feel very empowered to have a better understanding of how to access and use my brain more effectively.

I'm now looking forward to trading and earning money, which I can put to good use, giving me a much brighter and more rewarding outlook on life. I aim to have a brain MOT at least once a year now.

Solution

For this I will repeat the final paragraph of the comments from Les Meehan above and add his closing remarks:

The first step to resolving the self-worth limitations and learning that you do in fact deserve everything that you create in your life is to be aware of such past experiences and to resolve the emotional trauma they have created and which is still deep within you.

However, for fast and lasting resolution, this may require the assistance of an experienced external expert such as a behaviour coach. I am not saying this to drum up business but simply because I have the experience to know this is the case.

This passage is worth rereading because it provides a template for dealing with these issues, not only in trading but in life generally. You need to understand the root causes and then you can make progress.

This is a choice!

Section 6 – A Step-By-Step Guide to Trading Professionally

REMEMBER, THIS BOOK IS ALL ABOUT *THE BUSINESS OF TRADING*. IT IS not concerned mainly with theory, or market techniques, it is aimed fairly and squarely at a business approach, and business is all about profit and loss – essentially more of the former and less of the latter.

In business terms there are four key elements:

1. The **number of points** your trading systems make available over any period, net of losses.

2. The **number of points you actually pull in** (i.e. *Right Trading*).

3. The **size** you trade in (i.e. *Right Size*).

4. The **expenses** you incur. Generally these are fairly low and may just involve a price service, although many traders use free charts from the spread betting providers. However other traders can spend a lot of money on price services, news services, offices, assistants, etc.

Together these produce your profit; or, if you get it wrong, your loss.

For example, if your system produces 100 points, but you only capture 75 of those, and you trade at £50 per point, your profit is £3750.

On the other hand, if you manage a blinder and capture 120 points but trade at £10 per point you only get £1200.

Clearly your systems need to work but it is size which ultimately determines the scale of the success of your business.

Of course, there is an important factor which has a key effect on the size in which you can trade and this is *risk*.

In particular: how many points you risk on each trade.

For example, if you were to use the *ZeitGap* system you would be using a stop of 52 points but with a shorter-term system the stop may just be 10 points. This dramatically affects how much you risk on any one trade. At £10 per point the *ZeitGap* stop means you would be risking £520 (52 × £10 = £520) but if you were using a 10 point stop the risk at £10 per point is just £100 (10 × £10 = £100).

Assuming you are happy risking 4% on each trade and you have an account size of £12,500 you are fine with *ZeitGap* at £10 per point – you risk £520 which works out at 4.2% of £12,500.

But if you were only using a 10 point stop you could trade at £52 per point (10 × £52 = £520).

Of course, profitability is another issue but you need to keep your risk parameters under tight control.

In this section we are going to bring all this together.

A STEP-BY-STEP GUIDE TO SUCCESS

Before I start I want to make three points very clear:

1. **Research is a key part of trading success**. This is largely down to the individual trader. The more successful traders usually allocate time on a daily basis to researching new trading ideas and systems.

2. **Work on your trading psychology may be essential**.

3. It makes sense, as a business, to **target a certain level of income**. Given the nature of markets and the erratic nature of trading profits and losses this is easier said than done. However, it is possible to look back over your monthly results (I would actually suggest you prepare weekly and monthly reports on your results) and work out how many points you average on a weekly and/or monthly basis. With this information you can calculate the necessary trading size to give you the income you want. Here is an example:

    *   Points per month: 100

    *   Trading in sufficient size: I suggest £50 per point within 12 months

    *   Indicated income: £5000 per month

The first is dependent on honing your trading skills to make the most of market action. The second can raise psychological issues which you may need to work through. The third becomes your goal.

I use a broad quarterly timetable to gauge the progress of traders:

1. The first three months covers the learning process and traders should aim for FOCUS during this period together with the beginnings of STYLE.

2. After the second period of three months traders should have mastered RIGHT TRADING.

3. After the third period of three months traders should have mastered RIGHT SIZE.

4. At the end of the year traders should have made these WINNING HABITS.

Obviously you can vary this to your own requirements. The purpose of this section is to set out the principles so that you can do this yourself and this list of four stages makes up the structure of the section.

Are these realistic targets?

It can be tough to acquire solid trading skills, particularly if using longer-term strategies. But with shorter/medium-term strategies you get feedback far more regularly and you can therefore learn more quickly. As an example *ZeitGap* usually trades two or three times a week.

A lot of the error when human beings trade is do with the operation, *not* the plan. If you have traded for any length of time you will know what I am talking about. It is all too easy to bail out of a good position because of a small blip in the market. It's all too easy to take a small profit and avoid the bigger one just a short way down the road. It's all too easy to trade when you should not, for all the reasons I have outlined in this book.

You may want to think about mechanising some parts of your trading using …

Trading robots

If we use *ZeitGap* as an example, it is 100% mechanical and once I have the plan I find a robot is far more adept at simply following that plan than us humans. Robots do not suffer from emotional issues – at least not at this stage in their development.

Programming a robot takes a fair amount of work and I like to see evidence of success, meaning back-testing, forward-testing and live trading, before I commission the robot. Make sure you test robots thoroughly before going this route.

However once up and running it leaves the trader free to do more research and trade non-mechanical systems if desired.

Right now I have three trading robots in various degrees of readiness with more planned so it is early days but this is an area I expect to expand going forwards.

I will now look at each quarterly section in a little more detail.

THE FIRST THREE MONTHS – THE LEARNING PROCESS

If we take *ZeitGap* as an example then three months is plenty of time to absorb all the rules. More complex trading strategies may push this boundary.

During these three months the emphasis is on learning and position size is a secondary issue. Having said that those of you who have been trading for some years may already be comfortable with a decent size of trade.

If your trading goes well in this initial period I would suggest increasing size in any case.

In this period you will develop your FOCUS, albeit this will likely evolve as you go forwards, and you will also see the beginning of your STYLE.

If starting from scratch then this may take somewhat longer than three months.

THE SECOND THREE MONTHS – RIGHT TRADING

Once the first phase is out of the way the learning process will be practically complete. We can then enter the second phase where the emphasis is on RIGHT TRADING.

In real terms this means we trade the systems and extract from the market largely what it offers.

At the same time I suggest you do regular research and develop your own systems. These may be based on knowledge acquired during the initial phase. All traders usually find it far easier to trade systems they have themselves developed as they tend to develop systems that suit their own trading personality and, of course, they understand them thoroughly.

You may also increase size during this period but it is not the main issue.

FOCUS become more defined in this period, as does STYLE.

There is no reason why traders working alone cannot successfully complete this phase on their own, but I would encourage you to link up with a more experienced trader as a mentor if at all possible.

There is nothing like working with someone who has done it before to inspire confidence it can be done. I find successful people are only too happy to help those with the enthusiasm to succeed. You may also like to suggest helping out on research and trading as a way in. You will need to get on well together, as without that it will be an uphill struggle.

THE THIRD THREE MONTHS – RIGHT SIZE

This is where it gets interesting. This is when your trading can truly become a business and can start to support the lifestyle of your dreams.

I want to make it clear not everyone will achieve this goal. We all have elements of self-sabotage within us and the market is very adept at amplifying and exploiting all such weaknesses. For this reason I use Les Meehan, who I have mentioned earlier. Les has been very useful in helping a number of our clients overcome such obstacles.

In fact I think we all need this sort of input and I have taken sessions with Les myself – it is quite amazing what he can achieve!

It is my view that where there is a will there is a way but it can save months (years sometimes) to work with the right people. I wish this was something I had realised when I started out.

However, many people do not share these values. Many people feel that attending seminars is a dumb thing to do. They hold to this view even though many of the people attending seminars are prosperous and wealthy whereas almost all of the people who feel seminars are a waste of time are not prosperous and not wealthy – it is a funny old world.

You also have to be able to accept you can change, and not everyone is ready for that.

It is true that 90% of traders fail but this is exactly as it is with new business generally. I am told 85% of businesses fail in the first year or two and another 85% of those that last the first two years fail in the next few years.

By adopting this step-by-step approach you put yourself in a bracket more likely to succeed, but there are no guarantees.

One issue that becomes extremely important at this stage is Money Management. Money Management, at its essence, is all about never risking too much on any one trade.

For a free lesson in how this works you could do worse than try out the app '8 Ball Pool' which is an extremely realistic game of pool played on your smartphone or tablet. Beware, as the game is pretty addictive. You are always being tempted to get up to the next level by betting 50%+ of your available cash on games or tournaments.

You will find it does not matter how often you may win as you only need to lose once, and hit the inevitable string of losses, to find that your large pot of 10,000+ (or 100,000+) is down to sub-500 – as I have found on many occasions. It does not matter if this happens when playing an app like '8 Ball Pool', but it does when it is your real cash at stake.

In the earlier part of this book I outlined many of the issues that can trip up the wannabe trader. You might wonder why we can keep making the same mistakes over and over again and the reason comes down to the composition of the human brain, aka human psychology.

This is something I learnt from Les. When we are stressed it has a direct effect on the frontal lobe of the brain. The result is twofold. Firstly we lose the power of thought, and you may have experienced this. I know I have and suddenly I find I have done something without realising it.

Secondly we also lose our short-term memory: this usually means a few minutes but can mean an hour or so.

The reason the brain does this is for survival reasons. So if a man comes across a sabre-toothed tiger he does not waste time thinking but goes straight into action (fight or flight). However if he had passed a means of escape a few minutes before he may no longer remember it! At this point your emotions/instincts have taken over and are making the decisions rather than your logic. These emotions/instincts then drive your subsequent behaviours.

The way to overcome this is by training. The military know all about this sort of thing and train soldiers to react instinctively in a useful fashion. This is one way around stress; another is to become familiar with the situation you find yourself in.

The trading environment is controllable. You decide on how much you risk, how long you stay in the market, and the manner in which you trade. As these become a habit, stress levels reduce.

But if you then increase stakes you are suddenly outside of your comfort zone and stress can return – so you need to take care at this stage in the process.

The actual process of increasing stakes is simple; it merely involves entering a higher figure in a box and that controls your trading size. Behind this simple process you need to ensure:

1. That you are **not exceeding your Money Management parameters**, which may be in line with mine at 2% to 4%.

2. You have **sufficient capital** available – although it does not need to actually be in your trading account.

3. That you have got your **psychology under control** – this is much easier said than done.

BY THE END OF THE YEAR – A WINNING HABIT

By this point you have been through the whole process:

1. You have applied your FOCUS to acquire the knowledge you need and developed your systems and trading STYLE.

2. You have mastered RIGHT TRADING so you are getting a high percentage of the available points from your systems and trading.

3. You have increased size to RIGHT SIZE and should now be making a respectable, possibly substantial, income from your trading.

Human beings are creatures of habit and it is much better if those are winning habits.

Everyone is largely where they are in life because of their habits, from the beggars in the street, to those working in McDonald's, to those who have good jobs, to those at the top of the pile.

Developing a habit is not that difficult – you just need to keep doing the same thing again, again and again. Having said that, bad habits that have been built up over many years can sabotage your new habits, and it is quite easy to revert to type.

In order to avoid this you need to maintain discipline. You may well lapse from time to time and when you do you need to snap right back into line.

You will know when you get it wrong!

At such a point the worst thing that can happen is you make money by doing the wrong thing, reinforcing the bad habit.

Of course, if it is not *bad* then you are free to incorporate this new rule/behaviour as part of your system/methodology. Logic will dictate whether you should do this or not. A new technique whereby you throw Money Management out of the window if events X and Y happen is going to kill you over time and needs to be stamped out immediately.

A new technique whereby you add to a losing position on a *very* low risk basis if events A and B happen but never to the extent that your total risk exceeds 2% *may* make sense, especially if you carefully back-test this.

Flexibility is an important part of trading but only within a carefully constructed framework of risk control.

Conclusion

You may have noticed that internet marketing gurus often focus on publishing books and booklets with a view to you making your fortune.

This trend has been round for ages – the ancient Egyptians were probably doing exactly the same on papyrus! The simple premise is that we all have some talent and all we need to do is write about it.

There is an element of truth in this but the ability to write a whole book (or even a whole booklet) on your particular skill also has a lot to do with determination and perseverance – even though writing a whole book is actually far easier than most people think.

But having written your book the ability to actually *sell it* to enough people to fund your dream lifestyle is far harder, especially if it has a title like *The Joy Of Tarantulas*, which is the subject you happen to be a world authority on.

But who knows, maybe this will be next year's smash hit. In fact I have just found one with a similar title on Amazon! It gets truer and truer every day that anything we can imagine has probably already been done by someone somewhere.

Where do you want to go?

If you develop your abilities in the trading world then many people will want to know what you think.

When I say trading is a life skill this is one aspect of what I mean.

The ability to talk knowingly about the trading world and to extend that knowledge into the media by way of voice, the written word or video can open up whole new worlds of income to your trading career.

This may seem daunting to you. Most people place public speaking and death close in their order of their most feared events! But when I embark on a new venture I want to know *all* the options – every single way in which I can make sure I come out with a profit.

Of course you have to go further down the road to exploit this particular opportunity, but probably not as far as you might think – in fact it is more a matter of focus.

When I started trading full-time back in April 1987 my focus was 100% on the markets, and even though I published *The Technical Trader* from 1990 onwards my focus was still very much on the markets as I went on to manage money in the late 1990s.

In the noughties this changed as my trading took up less time and I became interested in new areas of human psychology and the internet; in fact I was interested in every aspect of a wider business and working with other traders.

You possibly have similar goals or maybe you have not thought about it – hence this section on advanced business thinking.

Some people, myself included at times, are very fond of saying "I can't do this …" and "I can't do that …" but in my experience you can do whatever you set out to do. Take writing (which is now a profitable sideline for me). I failed 'Use of English' at school – in fact it is the only exam I think I have ever failed! I was never much good at writing but now practice has taken me to a certain level.

In fact I believe I now write to a fairly high standard, albeit you can judge for yourself, and this is simply the result of doing something I *could not* do until I could. We have masses of experience of succeeding at this – when we were born we could not walk, talk or ride a bicycle.

So a trading system that gives you winning experiences in the market can lead down many other paths than simply those direct trading profits.

Maybe those profits are all you want, but it is good to be aware of other possibilities – in fact *it is one of the secrets of success*. The top entrepreneurs leave no stone unturned in their search for profit opportunities, whereas most others may occasionally stumble upon something they missed (possibly for the last ten years!) but they simply do not think in the same way.

Motivational speaker Stuart Goldsmith has this to say:

The money-making radar scan

You need to cultivate a radar scan for money-making opportunities. This comes very naturally to me and I have no idea if it can be taught or not. Basically wherever I am, I tend to be looking for business opportunities, or looking at an existing business and working out how they make their money.

I can't go to a restaurant without checking how many punters are there, what I reckon they are spending on average and what the overheads are. I then do a quick mental calculation and work out that there is, say, £175,000 profit in the business.

You need to be the same. There are dozens of opportunities out there as close to you as your skin. I expect you are completely blind to them at the moment as you drift through life in your normal half-asleep state. I'm not being rude. It's the human condition.

You need to start waking up and looking around you.

A very good friend of mine made £1m in property profits because he read a book (*Think like a Tycoon*) which told him to get on his bike and cycle around his local area looking for plots of land which could be developed. Unlike 99.99% of people reading that book, he went out immediately on his bike (yes, really) and identified a suitable plot of land. He didn't make £1m from that but he made enough to go on to make £1m from property over the next three years from a complete standing start.

Thousands of people walked right past that plot and barely glanced at it. The book fired up his radar scan for business opportunities and so within moments of cycling away from his home he spotted an opportunity.

You need to get in this zone too as often as you possibly can.

I couldn't agree more. Trading the markets is just one way of making money and you should be constantly on the lookout for others.

It always amuses me when some people criticise traders for being involved in other business activities, such as writing books, giving seminars, running services, etc. No one seems to criticise Apple for developing their products, or maximising the revenue and profits from their business. Apple had the Mac, why do they need iPads, iPods and iPhones?

Well, that is the nature of business. It provides opportunities and the good business will exploit those opportunities.

In fact I think it goes further than that. I believe we are all built to grow and evolve. It is natural we want to do this. The tragedy is that so many do not.

Money is only one consideration. Lifestyle is another and, personally, I enjoy working with clients and it makes life far more interesting and very satisfying when you help someone succeed!

In fact, taken to its logical conclusion, you do not need to trade at all and some make very good money out of the markets by developing trading systems and selling them, for example.

I have written this book for traders but the markets can help people make money in many, many ways.

Appendices

APPENDIX 1: THE XTREME STOP SYSTEM

This is one of my favourite systems and I use it more than any other, partly because it tends to form a part of my other systems, like *ZeitGap*.

Note: *Xtreme Stop* is a complete system in its own right.

I should mention this section is written to be complete in itself and so some points are covered which also appear elsewhere in this book; but as repetition is the essence of learning I make no apology for that.

The concept is very simple and is shown in the illustration below:

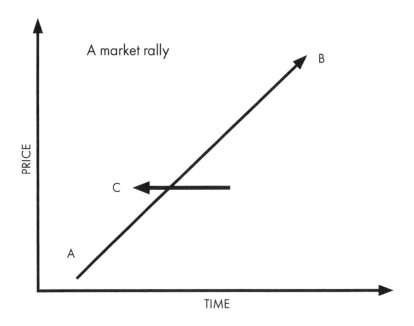

This shows a market rally which takes FTSE, or any other market, from point A to point B. The rally may be 50 points or it may be 500 points – the same principle applies – and the principle is that to get from point A to point B it must pass through point C.

The *Xtreme Stop* system provides a mechanism for jumping aboard at point C and taking the profit the market may offer.

To put this another way, *Xtreme Stop* is a method that gets you aboard a trend. It does this by picking a point (point C on the illustration above) within the trend (the trend being represented by the move from point A to point B).

The system will make money if you correctly identify the trend and you do not get stopped out.

Market orders

Before going any further I need to outline three types of market order and these are:

1. Trade at market

2. Stop

3. Limit

The first, trade at market, means you simply trade at the price offered by the trading or betting platform. If, say, IG Index tells you that FTSE is trading at 5763.5/5764.5 (see following screenshot) then if you click on the arrow to the left, those are the prices you can trade at (although as they change virtually every second there will be some small changes – and very occasionally some not so small changes).

To put this more succinctly: a market order is transacted as quickly as possible at the best prevailing price.

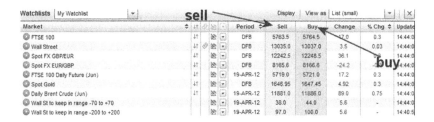

If we look at the IG price of 5763.5/5764.5 you will see we can *sell* at the lower figure and *buy* at the higher figure (if we could do the reverse we would immediately be in front and, sadly, the world does not work that way). The difference between the sell and buy prices is the *spread* and this is one of the ways in which the betting platform makes money.

Stops and limits work differently. When you trade at market the trade (bet) is effected immediately (unless you hit liquidity issues when trading in size) but with stops and limits *the market has to move before your trade can take place*.

This is because with a *limit* you are seeking a better price than the current market price:

- If you wish to **buy** the market (place an UP bet) a better price means a lower price than the current market price.

- If you are **selling** (placing a DOWN bet) it means a *higher* price.

Stops work in the opposite direction. With a stop you are looking to get a worse price, so when *buying* the stop price is higher than the current market price, and when *selling* it is lower.

Before going further let me first deal with an area of confusion that can arise. The expression *stop* is generally used in connection with the idea of protecting an existing position (a stop loss) and a stop does indeed do this. So you may *buy* the market (up bet) and then place a stop lower down to protect yourself. If the market then falls back, the stop will come into effect so that any loss you make will be small and controlled – all losses should be small in the context of your trading capital and, as you choose your own stop level, this is your choice.

However a stop is simply a type of market order and you can use it how you wish. *Xtreme Stop* uses the stop order to *enter* positions.

Now, you may wonder why we want to use a stop to enter at a worse price than we can get right away by trading at market.

Good question!

This goes to the heart of the *Xtreme Stop* system. In fact it comes back to that diagram with the market moving between points A and B. Remember it has to pass through point C on the way?

The key phrase is pass through because we want to pick point C with some care. We never know for sure that the market will reach point B, but look at any price chart of any market and you will see it is *always* moving between points A and B. To add to our chances of success we want it to pass through C.

For example, what happens if the market, say FTSE, does not pass through point C?

Well, in that case it is *never* going to reach point B! So do we really want to trade?

Well, guess what …

We don't – because the system requires that the market passes through point C. In this case that never happens; so no trade.

This is one major advantage of this system and it is an important one.

Consistent trading profits are a balance between the profits you make and the losses you make (losses are inevitable and anyone who tells you otherwise is either a knave or a fool).

There is no reason to take more losses than you have to, just as there is no reason to take big losses – *Xtreme Stop* does all this for you.

Plus when it does bag a profit it can be *big*!

It is also a very easy system to operate. Here is a step-by-step guide:

Step-by-step guide to Xtreme Stop

1. Choose your market.

2. Decide where this market may go (i.e. in which direction you want to trade, up or down).

3. Choose point C.

4. Place your stop to enter the market if it passes through point C (if it doesn't, nothing will happen and your order will not be executed).

5. Place another stop to bail out if the trade goes wrong (this will keep your losses small). This is the traditional stop loss and it's a stop to exit if things get rough.

6. Optionally place a limit to take your profits. (Again this is automatic once set. If the market hits your limit level you'll be taken out with that amount of profit.)

Now let me explain all that.

Step 1: Choose your market

Some traders specialise in one market, for example the UK FTSE. Others, like myself, trade a small range of markets; I have had success with *Xtreme Stop* on FTSE, the US Dow, the German DAX, Gold and GBP/EUR. Others may trade whatever they lay their eyes on.

Xtreme Stop will work with any market that moves from point A to point B and I have yet to find a market that does not do that.

Time frame is one key factor because you can look at a chart of the daily action, perhaps composed of price bars showing the whole day's price movement with the high at the top, the low at the bottom with the opening level marked to the left and the closing level marked to the right – each bar will look like this:

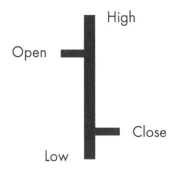

A chart comprising such bars looks like this:

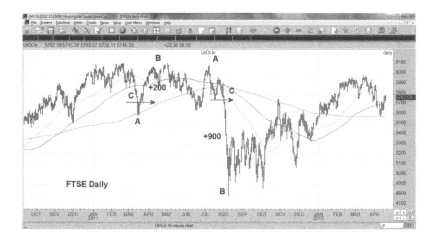

If you look at the chart above you will see I have marked a couple of A – B moves and also entered levels for C at daily highs/lows which would have worked extremely well!

Here is a 5-minute chart:

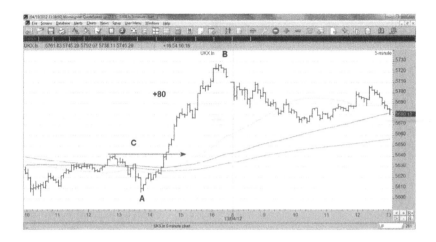

Hopefully you can see the same opportunities appear.

So you are free to choose a market and time frame of your choice and there are many, many to choose from. My suggestion would be to check out a few charts and find a market that is moving around (has good volatility) – *Xtreme Stop needs movement to work.*

Step 2: Decide direction

One of the key trading rules is the trend is your friend; this means that moves that are in force tend to continue. The following chart of gold is a good example offering many chances to profit from *Xtreme Stop.*

The chart covers a period of around 20 months from July 2009 to March 2011 and you can see gold was in a solid uptrend during that period.

Gold is a market that tends to trend, both up and down, regularly and you may want to watch gold when considering *Xtreme Stop*.

You don't need any fancy technical indicators to tell you that you should be looking to buy the market shown above – you just need to look at it to see it is going up!

You will see that I have marked numerous point Cs on the chart and all of these gave good profit potential.

Exactly how much profit you make will depend on your exit strategy and this we will be discussing shortly – clearly to bag your profit you must both enter and exit. Any good system will cover both of these vital functions.

I have also marked one C on the chart as C** – this is the highest C on the chart and is pretty close to the right-hand side. This is an example of a C (trigger point) that would not be triggered. In this case it was because the market went down and it was superseded by a C lower down.

This was a good thing too as you would have been buying at a high that was not exceeded for two months or so – a good example of avoiding a losing trade.

But you will need to be careful with these Cs that don't get triggered. Stops can be placed GTC (Good Till Cancelled); if you leave your stops to enter in place you may find you suddenly enter a position, days, weeks, or months down the road which you had forgotten all about!

There are three ways around this:

1. On IG you can place stops and specify when the order expires.

2. Other betting sites usually have similar options and on Ayondo (formerly Gekko), for example, you can place stops good for the day only.

3. Regularly, preferably daily, review your open orders and cancel those that are no longer applicable.

I recommend the third option.

In fact I *have* been triggered into trades I should have cancelled – so far I am up on these. Nevertheless it cannot be considered best practice. *You have been warned.*

There is one final and vital point to make on this chart of gold. At this point I am keeping this as straightforward as possible so that you understand how *Xtreme Stop* works. As such I have not marked losing Cs on the chart. But make no mistake about it, not all your trades will be winners – *there will be losses.*

Step 3: Choose point C

First let me restate how the system works.

You pick a market extreme, meaning a *high or low* that you consider important, and place a stop to enter beyond that extreme. In other words, if the market breaches that extreme high or low, your order to enter is automatically triggered.

So let's say the market of your choice (maybe the UK FTSE 100 Index) has seen a high at 5200 and you feel a breakout above that level might lead to a solid rally – in fact you may have been looking for an entry point for such a rally. So you add a few points, say 3, and place a *stop to buy* order at 5203.

The market then moves through your stop and triggers you long (places your UP bet). Here is an illustration of how it works ...

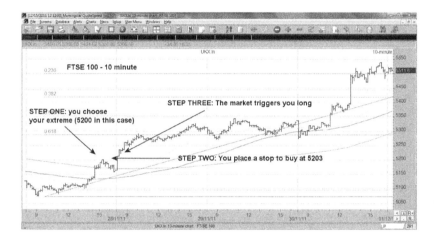

Let's just go through that in a little more detail.

You choose an extreme. In this case we choose a high made by a rally that is already in place, but we can choose from a number of different extremes. For example, I often use the opening range of a market (i.e. the extreme high and low made in the first hour of trading, or even the first ten minutes sometimes).

You place your stop to enter the market. As I have already said, a stop is the name given to a market order which is only triggered if the market goes beyond a certain point. Stops are generally known as ways of controlling risk, meaning that they are generally used to exit trades once the trade goes against you to a pre-determined point. But here we are using the stop to *open* a position.

The market moves and in fact it may never hit your stop and you may never enter, but if you *do* enter then you can look at your open profit.

There is more to this, but not a huge amount more. First I want to tell you why I really like this system ...

The *big* advantage of *Xtreme Stop* is that it will catch *every* move.

Another biggie is that unless the market moves through your stop you never enter – if you traded before that level was penetrated you would probably lose money and a system that only enters on a breakout has value for that reason.

Of course there will be losses – false breakouts are fairly common and it's annoying when your stop to enter *just* gets triggered only to see the market then immediately turn against you!

Here is a Camtasia clip I recorded on this system showing it in action: **www.johnpiper.info/xtremestop.wmv**

Additional articles and videos are available on my website. Please visit **twtt.johnpipersupport.com** and enter the password BOOK26.

When choosing point C the key aim is to get aboard a good move and examining the previous price history is a good guide.

Step 4: Place your stop to enter at point C

I suggest using a small adjustment of 3 or 4 points – although this is a factor you should personalise to suit your taste.

I have already said that I suggest using a high or a low (i.e. an extreme) for point C and you will *add* this adjustment to a high and *deduct* it from a low.

We will now look at how you enter your trading instruction using the platform offered by IG Index; here is the first screenshot explaining this process:

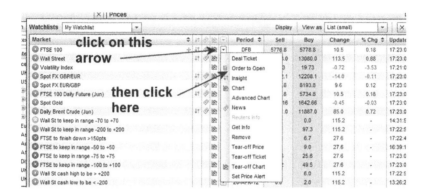

You click on the arrow and the box appears. You then click on 'Order to Open' and you will see the following (which allows you to place both stops and limits):

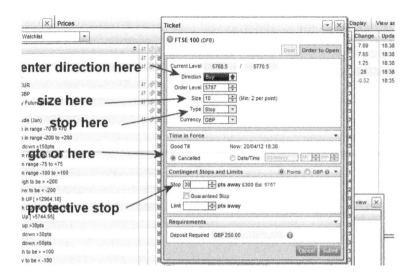

Having entered all the key information in the box simply click on *Submit* which is the button in the bottom right-hand corner of the box.

The website will confirm that your order has been accepted and you will also find the order listed under *Working Orders*. If triggered the trade will then be shown under *Open Positions*.

Step 5: Place your protective stop

Remember: this is the stop to get you out of the action if the market moves against you.

There are variations in how different betting sites allow you to place these.

On the IG site, as above, you enter the distance away from your entry point. This has some advantages and some disadvantages. The main advantage is that you always know *how much you are risking* in that it is always x points away from your entry. The main disadvantage is that if you choose your stop based on previous market action, as I do, the stop will shift depending on your actual entry point.

This may sound a little complex but it all comes down to something called *slippage*. To explain this let's take the order level in the screenshot above.

I have entered the stop to enter the order level at 5787 and the protective stop as 30 points away. As this order is to *buy* the market the stop will be *below* the market and 5787 less 30 is 5757. Now let's assume 5760 is a level on the market you consider important, perhaps because the market has bounced off that level a few times. A level of this sort is known as support – a break below such levels is what *Xtreme Stop* is all about. Similarly a level which the market is having trouble moving above is known as resistance. If you consider 5760 as a support level you may want it between the level at which you open your position and the stop level.

Now let's assume the market moves through 5787 but it moves real fast and the stop to enter is actually triggered at 5793 – that is 6 points of slippage. This happens sometimes in fast-moving markets but it is very rare that slippage is more than 1 or 2 points. Now I have a problem as my stop at 30 points away is now at 5763 and that support level no longer gives my stop any protection.

So I prefer the method other platforms employ (ETX offers both) whereby you enter the absolute stop level you want (e.g. 5757), not the distance away from your entry. The disadvantage here is that you may find the amount you are risking is a little more than you had expected (because of possible slippage), but I feel it is more important to have some reason for placing the stop where you want it.

Having said that, you are always free to adjust stops after the event so if you use IG and are not happy with where the stop ends up you can change it.

To summarise, I would suggest placing your stop at least 30 or 40 points away for the FTSE (this will vary with the market traded) and ideally beyond support or resistance. As ever, when testing out any new system I suggest paper trading initially and then only risking smaller sums until you have proven the concept.

Step 6: Set up a limit to take profits

This is optional and brings up another area you may want to consider. There are primarily three ways in which to take your profits (exit the markets) and these are:

1. You take them when you feel like it, which is somewhat arbitrary and is unlikely to give you the most bang for your buck. It is also an emotional roller coaster and can make you grab small profits and leave losses running as you wait for the market to turn back in your favour.

2. You follow the market with your stop, so as more profit builds up, you tighten the stop to lock in ever increasing amounts. This is a good strategy and allows you to make big killings from time to time when you catch large moves. But you should always be careful to place stops where they have some meaning (for example beyond support or resistance, always being aware that the market knows we do this!).

3. You use profit targets and set automatic limit orders to exit when that amount of profit has been made.

The first option above is always fraught with the risk of throwing away the value of your labour. It is all too easy to see a small, yet appealing, profit sitting there just waiting to be taken.

It is always better to have a plan.

Having said that it is important to follow your own lights. *Xtreme Stop* is designed to catch moves and the rules for doing this are fairly precise. However this trading system is not 100% mechanical and it allows you to use your discretion. Maybe that is why I like it so much.

OK, that covers *Xtreme Stop* and we are now moving to *ZeitGap*.

APPENDIX 2: THE ZEITGAP SYSTEM

We are now going to look at the basic ideas behind *ZeitGap;* this section is formed of the first two of the eleven *ZeitGap* modules.

As *ZeitGap* is a precise trading system it would prejudice the profitability of the system to show it all in a book of this type. Plus my paying customers would not be too happy!

However, these two sections do outline the trading idea. As such you may find this section a very valuable resource offering much food for thought as to research ideas.

Introduction

One of the wonderful things about *ZeitGap* is how simple it is to understand and operate. For example, we only look at one index, the German *DAX*.

All we do is place simple trades on which way the DAX is going to move. We aim to be right more often than we are wrong and hence make steady profits.

It really is that easy.

Previously *ZeitGap* was called *KrautGap*

I want to say a quick word about the previous name of this system. I am not trying to be offensive to my German friends! Rather the opposite. I like Krautrock music and the term Kraut is used endearingly in that context.

Since this system concerns the German DAX Index, and since it is a gap-trading system (to be explained) the name *KrautGap* sprang to mind. I liked it, so it stayed, that is until it got hit by the PC brigade! Only one person actually objected to the name, and that was on behalf of his wife who had made no comment. Anyway, the end result: *KrautGap* became *ZeitGap*.

The trading idea

In this section I am going to introduce what I call the trading idea and by this I mean the pattern of market action on which we base our trading system.

What we are looking for (what every successful trader needs) is an edge.

In order to introduce this idea I am going to show you a chart of price action. This chart shows you what this system is all about:

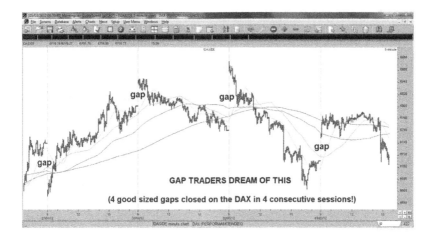

Don't panic if this is all completely new to you. I want to make this understandable to seasoned traders *and* to absolute beginners, so bear with me if some things are obvious to you (remember how you struggled when you started out).

So let me walk you through the chart, nice and slowly.

The first thing to notice is that it is a chart of the DAX – the index of the German stock market. It's the German equivalent of the FTSE.

Now look at the bottom axis and notice it covers a period approximately from 27 April 2012 to the close of play on 3 May 2012 – four trading sessions.

The right-hand vertical axis is, of course, the level of the DAX index.

So far so good.

Spotting gaps

Now I want to draw your attention to the gaps.

A gap is when the index takes a sudden jump up or down in value, with no intervening price bars.

I'm sure you can see when this will happen most frequently. It's when the market closes for the day at one level, and then something happens overnight (usually good or bad news) and then when the market opens first thing in the morning, it is sharply higher or lower than the previous close, leaving a gap in the price chart. Actually sometimes nothing at all happens overnight but that's markets for you! (In fact it is often these moves which are the most interesting.)

I'm sure you can easily spot the four gaps in the chart above. They are at:

- 9am (the open) on 27/4/12
- 9am (the open) on 30/4/12
- 9am (the open) on 2/5/12
- 9am (the open) on 3/5/12

Don't go further until you're completely happy with being able to spot these four gaps.

Notice how all four gaps are on the morning open of the index. That's where I said most of them would be … and there they are.

As you will have worked out by now, our objective is to profit from these gaps.

The main idea behind *ZeitGap* is deceptively simple. In fact I can state it in four words:

Gaps tend to close.

What do I mean by that?

Well, I expect you're onto this already but let me spell it out. The theory is this: if a nice, big gap opens up, over the course of time (minutes, hours or sometimes days) the gap tends to close – in other words *the index often retraces the direction of the gap.*

- If the gap is sharply **upwards**, over time the index drifts back *downwards.*

- If the gap is sharply **downwards**, over time the index drifts back *upwards.*

These gaps keep closing!

Let's go back and have a look at the chart of the DAX above.

27 April 2012

First look at 9am on 27 April 2012. You can see a big downward gap. The index closed at about 6740 on the previous day (26 April 2012) and opened sharply downwards at about 6660 on the 27th.

But look what happened then!

The index retraced its lost ground until, a mere one hour later, it was back at 6740 again.

30 April 2012

Now look at the smaller gap on 30 April 2012 at 9am. The index closed at about 6800 on the previous day and opened sharply upwards at about 6840 on the 30th.

But what happened next?

Again, in about one hour the index lost all that ground and found itself back at 6800 again.

2 May 2012

Let's look at the next one on 2 May 2012. Again at 9am. The previous close was at about 6755 but the opening on 2 May was massively higher at 6875. Hard to make up that ground, you may be thinking? But look how the chart drifts downwards until just over three hours later it is back again at 6755 having closed the gap!

3 May 2012

Finally let's look at the gap on 3 May 2012.

The close on 2 May 2012 was about the 6710 level. The opening the following morning (3 May 2012) was sharply higher at about 6750. Now this gap took a bit longer to close, but close it did. By 3pm on the same day, the index had lost all the points gained by the upward spiking gap and had reached 6710 once again.

Now, I *hope* you're thinking:

> Hmmm … I like the look of this. If I see a gap and then bet the *opposite way* to that gap, over time the gap will close and I'll make lots of money.

And you would be right, because that is the basic idea behind *ZeitGap*.

Again, please don't go any further until you have understood the theory behind making money from this which is: wait for a gap, bet the opposite way, watch the gap close, make a profit.

Of course it does not always work that way. Not all gaps close and the system does lose. This is why we need to test out any trading idea. Most ideas work, in the sense they will capture the profits around which the idea is based, *but* you need to check out the downside: how much the system loses when the idea does not work.

At that point many ideas fall by the wayside.

Why the DAX?

I want to briefly address something you might be thinking:

Why the DAX, why don't we do this on the FTSE?

The answer is that the gaps in the FTSE are hidden and it *always* opens at the previous day's close (in fact this is artificial and the true opening level is usually different but you cannot see that on the FTSE chart). That's why we use the DAX. Actually there is more to it than that. The DAX is far more dynamic, meaning we make more money more quickly *and* it is better at closing gaps!

Now I have to say straightaway that the chart above is exceptional. Four nice big gaps of which three were closed directly after the opening and the third closed later in the day – that equals profit in any language!

Having said this, it is not that rare to see a chart like this and there are often plenty of nice gaps for us to profit from.

With this system you get steps that are 100% mechanical so you know exactly what to do every day. This does not mean the system has to be completely inflexible though and you may well find yourself improving the system so that it suits your trading style more precisely. But when starting out I suggest you just follow my simple steps and gain experience (and in the trading world experience equals success, as long as you follow the rules!).

Gap theory – more on gaps

I'm going to talk some more about gaps, because the topic is important.

Say a market closes at one level, 6000, and then opens at another level, say 6050. This means there is no trading between 6000 and 6050 – this is a gap and rather as nature abhors a vacuum, a market abhors a gap and tends to close it as soon as possible.

Why?

Because the job of the market is to maximise trade, rather as our job on earth is to maximise our individual potential. And at every price point between 6000 and 6050 there will be traders willing to trade and the market wants that action!

For this reason most gaps close and this gives us a great opportunity. If the market opens at 6050 we need only *sell* and we would then close the trade and win if the gap is closed at 6000. If the market opens lower, say at 5950, we need only *buy* and we would then close the trade and win if the gap is closed at 6000.

That is our trading idea and it's a good one.

Gaps have been tested over the years and they are highly reliable. Roughly 70% to 80% of gaps close and that means you will generally make money on 70% to 80% of your trades – much better than most other systems!

However markets can be tricky and so I will be covering a number of key techniques which will prove highly useful in extracting cash from the markets.

Hidden gaps

I touched on this before and now I want to say a bit more about something that is quite odd about gaps – they are usually hidden! I have chosen one of the few indices (the DAX) and one of the few charts of that index which actually shows the gaps.

If you use your spread betting company's charts the gaps vanish.

Why?

Because they use 24-hour charting and there are very few gaps left visible. Plus if you look at major indices like the FTSE 100 and the DOW you will *never* see gaps because these indices artificially open at the previous closing level. The gaps are hidden!

In my view this is deliberate. Professional traders use gaps because they are very reliable, so why leave them lying around for anyone to see? Much better to hide them away. This really is buried treasure!

Exercise – finding the gaps

This brings us to your homework for this section, which is designed to meet two objectives:

1. To get you familiar with looking at price charts and seeing gaps.

2. To get you thinking about how to trade the gaps.

There are four steps involved:

Step 1

This is based on the German DAX Index and the first step is to establish where the DAX closed the night before. There are various ways in which you can do this.

First you need to know the trading hours. As the DAX is a German Index the timings are in CET (Central European Time) which is generally one hour ahead of UK time. The DAX Index:

*   **Opens** at 09h00 CET each morning, which is usually 08h00 in the UK.

*   **Closes** at 17h30 CET, which is usually 16h30 in the UK.

The DAX basically trades the same hours as the UK FTSE 100 Index.

However one point to note is that it can take a minute or two before official prices come through after the open at 09h00 CET.

You will find the DAX on free services like:

*   **ADVFN (www.advfn.com)** – on ADVFN the full name is DAX Performance Index.

*   **Yahoo Finance (finance.yahoo.com)** – the symbol here is ^GDAXI and the URL is **finance.yahoo.com/q?s=^GDAXI**.

Personally, I use Yahoo Finance and suggest you do the same.

So, after the close, establish the closing level – make a clear note of this (obviously a spreadsheet is the best way to record this). You'll also need to add the date.

Step 2

The next step is to watch the open just after 09h00 CET (08h00 in the UK) and simply note the opening level. It is probably easiest to watch this via your spread betting company – I recommend IG Index and Ayondo. In fact you could also use this for the closing level, but it is better to use the official closing level as shown on Yahoo Finance.

Step 3

Now calculate the *difference* between the previous day's close and the following day's open.

Step 4

Now check whether the gap has been closed. Obviously you'll have to wait a while to see what happens.

Results

The table below sets out below my own results of doing this test in June 2012.

Date (2012)	Closing Level	Opening Level (next day)	Difference	Was gap closed?
1 June	6264	6259	5	11 June
4 June	6050	5976	74	6 June
5 June	5978	5999	21	YES!
6 June	5969	6028	59	
7 June	6093	6117	24	8 June
8 June	6144	6082	62	YES!
11 June	6130	6255	125	YES!
12 June	6141	6141	0	YES!

Date (2012)	Closing Level	Opening Level (next day)	Difference	Was gap closed?
13 June	6161	6183	22	YES!
14 June	6152	6146	6	YES!
15 June	6138	6164	26	25 June
18 June	6229	6304	75	YES!
19 June	6248	6254	6	YES!
20 June	6363	6364	1	YES!
21 June	6392	6357	35	YES!
22 June	6343	6273	70	29 June
25 June	6263	6229	34	29 June
26 June	6132	6157	25	YES!
27 June	6136	6155	19	YES!
28 June	6228	6232	4	YES!
29 June	6149	6296	147	

Here's the exciting thing: every row with a YES! is a profit you could have taken that day!

It is only when there is no entry in the final column that there is no profit opportunity (because the gap did not close, at least not that month, but 95%+ of gaps close at some point).

In a normal month you will find that the majority of entries are a clear YES! with most of the rest having a date in them. Only a very few will be left blank. The date in column 5 tells us the gap was closed, but not on the same day it opened.

In June 2012, as you can see above, we had 13 days marked YES! out of a total 21 days. Of these 5 were small gaps which we probably wouldn't trade. The total profit from the remaining 8 days amounts to **384 points**.

You may think that this is a waste of your time but you are in the process of acquiring a life skill which will stand you in good stead for many months and years to come. The reason to do this is that it is important that you see how good this system can be in a typical month. This underlies your future success.

Incidentally I repeated this exercise in July 2015 and got a very similar result – 388 points, 4 more! *ZeitGap* is passing the test of time very well!!

Trading rules

Earlier in this book I mentioned the three key trading rules:

1. Cut your losses

2. Run your profits

3. Trade selectively

I want to briefly revisit the first and third of these and see how they relate to the system we're currently looking at.

Cut your losses

This rule simply means you never lose more than a small or acceptable sum. The mechanism for this seeming miracle is something called a **stop**, whereby you exit at a predetermined point if the trade goes against you.

You will have noticed when we did the exercise above that most of the gaps were closed the same day but some took days to close, and some did not close at all. You may have wondered what would have happened if you had traded on these days.

Well you *could* have been exposed to a large loss if you did not take certain precautions. For example, you could have bet the market would close the gap in the downwards direction, but it just kept rising … and rising … and rising. Obviously this would expose you to huge losses.

But relax! Good trading practice does not allow this to happen and this is where **stops** come in (which I'm going to come back to soon).

Trade selectively

The third rule added the icing to the cake. It involves learning which are the better trades and only taking them. If you only take the best trades then you achieve a double whammy – you get better profits and you eliminate more losses.

As an example let's look back at the results of the gap exercise. When I did this in June 2012, there were a number of YES! days with very small gaps, let's say less than 11 points. If we ignored those we would hardly lose much. In fact on one of those days – 1 June – it was only 5 points and that gap was not closed until 11 June (ten days later)!

In fact the DAX moved over 300 points in the wrong direction before closing that gap. At £10 per point that is over £3000 risked in an attempt to win 5 points (£50). Of course it would not have been a risk had we known the gap was definitely going to close, but we didn't know that at the time. For all we knew we were £3,000 down and that was just the start of our losses!

But don't worry, if you follow the rules you will never experience such a loss as this. It is completely impossible. The full system includes a number of ways of filtering out the trades we do not want whilst limiting losses when trades go against us.

Let's now look at how we can use stops with the *ZeitGap* system.

Using stops with ZeitGap

Let's start with a couple of examples.

Example 1: How to place a stop with an UP gap

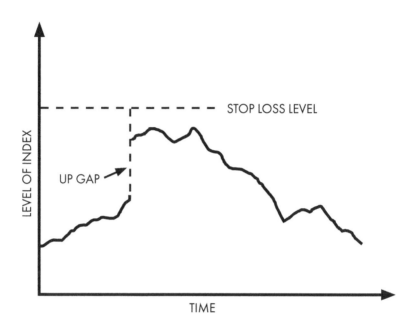

If the DAX opens **above** the prior close (an UP GAP) we **sell** the market (bet it will go DOWN) and profit if the market goes **down**. To protect ourselves and ensure our loss is small and acceptable we place our stop **above** our entry point to cover the case where the market continues to rise. So if the DAX closes at 6000 the day before and then opens at 6050, we **sell** at 6050 with a view to taking 50 points out of the market if the DAX falls to 6000 and closes the gap.

We can choose where to place the stop and we place it **above** our entry to protect us if the market goes the wrong way – of course the market is never wrong but you know what I mean! If we were to place it at 6075 we would be risking 25 points; at 6100 we would risk 50 points.

Breaking this down, if the market continued up 25 points we would get taken out automatically with a 25 point loss. At £2 a point we would have lost £50. Or, if we placed our stop 50 points above, and the market traded up through this level, again we would get taken out automatically with a 50 point loss. At £2 a point our loss would be £100.

Example 2: How to place a stop with a DOWN gap

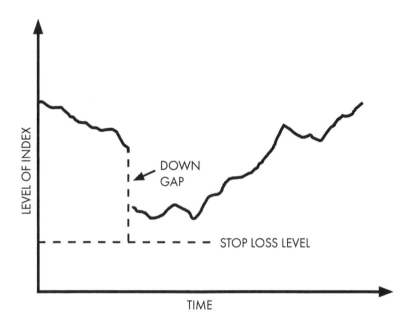

Similarly, if the DAX opens **below** the prior close (a DOWN GAP) we **buy** the market (bet it will go UP) and profit if the market goes **up**. To protect ourselves and ensure our loss is small and acceptable we place our stop **below** our entry point. So if the DAX closes at 6000 the day before and then opens at 5950, we **buy** at 5950 with a view to taking 50 points out of the market if the DAX rallies to 6000 and closes the gap.

Again, we can choose where to place the stop and we place it below our entry. If we were to place it at 5925 we would be risking 25 points; at 5900 we would risk 50 points.

Selecting the best stop level

As I've mentioned before, choosing the stop level is a trade-off between minimising the amount you lose when the stop is hit and minimising the number of times the stop is hit.

Choosing the stop level comes down to testing different levels in the market and there is a fair amount of work in this – which, of course, I have done for you.

The result of all this effort is 52, and so that is the stop we use.

Looking back at our examples above:

- In example 1 we **sold** at 6050. When we sell we want the market to go down because then we win. As such the stop needs to be at a *higher* level to cover us if the market goes the wrong way (i.e. up). So our stop here will be at 6102 (6050 + 52 = 6102).

- In example 2 we **bought** at 5950. When we buy we want the market to go up because then we win. As such the stop needs to be at a *lower* level to cover us if the market goes the wrong way (i.e. down). So our stop here will be at 5898 (5950 - 52 = 5898).

Just to make the point clear, if either stop was hit we would lose 52 points. At £2 a point this would be £104. At £1 a point it would be £52.

Exercise – using stops

Look back at the previous exercise and see how many of your YES! trades would have been stopped out by using a 52 point stop – to do this you will need to re-examine each day's chart.

Don't worry about the other days at this point.

To explain your task a little more fully, the object of this exercise is to look at each YES! trade to see which of these it did first. Either the market:

1. Closed the gap, or

2. Moved 52 points in the wrong direction.

In a normal month you will find very few trades get stopped out (i.e. very few trades go 52 points the wrong way).

That concludes the short introduction to *ZeitGap*. The full system is available at **www.zeitgap.com**.

APPENDIX 3: THE TRADING EXPERIENCE, AN EMOTIONAL ROLLER COASTER BY LES MEEHAN

I am including this article by Les Meehan primarily because it expands on a number of topics discussed within the body of this book. Further, in *The Way to Trade* I included *The Troubled Trader* by Tony Plummer (who was kind enough to write the foreword to this book) and as I see this as the next book in the series I wanted to maintain the same structure. I think you will enjoy it!

About this article

In writing this article, I [Les Meehan] have assumed you have experienced the emotional side of trading and decided that you now want to be more in control of the emotional aspects of trading. Also, that you are ready to create some positive change in yourself and actively make your trading more successful.

This article is an introduction to several of the key aspects of human psychology that have a direct impact on your trading experience.

By reading each section and applying what you learn to your own mind and behaviours you will get to know yourself and bring into your awareness several of the emotional drivers that may be adversely affecting your trading.

Also, by simply doing the little exercises I have provided for you, the solutions to some of your challenges may reveal themselves and give you an opportunity to change and grow.

Disclaimer: By reading further you agree and accept that the author cannot be held liable or responsible for how you use the content of this article.

So, get ready to journey into you!

[NB For the full article with pictures, additional articles and videos please visit **twtt.johnpipersupport.com** and enter the password BOOK26 (upper case).]

The Trading Experience – an emotional roller coaster

Welcome to the world of your trading emotions! This article is an introduction to The Trading Experience Emotional Roller Coaster. If you have been trading for a while, or even if you are new to trading, you will no doubt already have some experience of riding your own emotional roller coaster that is trading. Whether that ride has so far been smooth or quite bumpy for you, this article will explore some of the ups and downs of your experience to assist you to understand not only more about your trading experiences but also more about YOU!

So, jump aboard and join me for a more leisurely ride into the world of your trading emotions.

Note: I am not writing this article as a scientific treatise but as a readable and easy to understand introduction to a very complex subject – YOU! Therefore, in discussing how the human brain and body work I have adopted the KISS (Keep It Short & Simple) principle in my explanations of complex topics. This is my usual style of writing so everyone can easily understand what I am saying.

Emotions – what are they anyway?

Of course we all experience emotion every single moment we are alive so it may seem an odd question to ask: *what are emotions?*

Even though we experience emotions all of the time, not many people actually understand them and the mechanism that creates them; and even fewer people know how to control them!

At the most basic level we can say:

> The emotion we are experiencing in any given moment is a combination of what we are thinking together with what we are feeling in our body.

An emotion then is the sum of our psychological and physiological states at any one time.

A *psychological state* can be said to be what we are thinking: our thoughts, the voices in our mind, the images we create, the sounds we make, all add up to produce our mental state. If not controlled these can, and often do, produce mind noise which makes it hard to think clearly. Of course this is very much an over-simplification of what is a very complex set of processes going on in the brain but this is not a medical textbook so for the purpose of this article I'm keeping it simple and easy!

A *physiological state* is mainly dictated by our body chemistry – that complex soup that keeps us functioning and which we can feel when we tune in to it. It is this chemical soup that produces what we physically feel in our bodies. When we feel great and can take on the world the soup has a higher quantity of, let's call them, friendly chemicals, whereas when we feel down the soup has too many unfriendly chemicals in it. Whatever the balance is of these various friendly and unfriendly chemical ingredients that are producing the soup, the final mix is a reflection of the context you are in and the response your mind/body determines is the best preparation for dealing with that context.

Of course both of these states, the mental processes and the chemical soup, whether friendly or not, have their purposes and one of these is to make you aware of yourself and your reaction to your environment – including the people and things in that environment.

Understanding your own states is a vital part of self-awareness, which is an important skill to develop for controlling your emotions and your trading experience.

Why are emotions important in trading?

If you have even the slightest experience of trading you will have had at least a short ride on the emotional roller coaster – and what was that like for you?

Whether it was a thrilling high or a plunging low, or something in between, you have probably been left in no doubt that emotions play a role in your trading experience.

So why are emotions important in trading? Well, it comes right back to how your brain functions and that chemical soup I put on the menu earlier.

Your brain

The easiest way to discuss the human brain is to imagine it has three major parts. In order of evolutionary development these are:

1. The Cerebellum: rear part of the brain

This is the survival or reptilian part and includes the brain stem (spinal cord). It is believed this part developed first in all reptiles and mammals. The reptile brain controls essential bodily functions and also keeps you safe from danger using what we refer to as our survival instinct (often called the fight or flight reaction).

2. The Limbic: middle part of the brain

This is the emotional part that heavily influences behaviours and is the main structure of our trading emotional roller coaster and the main topic of this article. It is also responsible for our judgement system which is why we often make judgements about things, like buying a new outfit to wear, and then later when logic returns we wonder why we did it. Salespeople love the limbic brain because they know we buy with this rather than with our logical mind.

3. The Neocortex: the two frontal lobes of the brain

This part is responsible for language, logic, imagination, and consciousness.

If you could only use the neocortex in your trading then I wouldn't have needed to write this article; unfortunately this is not the case.

Since we are human beings rather than trading robots, these three parts of our brain function together rather than independently.

It is how they function together that either helps you in your trading or sets you riding the emotional roller coaster.

How the brain parts function

Let's keep our KISS explanations going as we take a simplified but useful look at how the three parts of your brain interact to help you function.

Whenever we have a new experience our senses take in information from that experience so fast that we are not even aware of it at first. This information is passed to the thalamus in the reptile brain because we need to know if there is danger to our survival – we use our amygdala, or survival instinct, to test the new experience. You can become aware of the speed of this process by recalling how fast your startle response is to a sudden unexpected noise or movement.

The information is also passed to your sensory cortex, which applies some thinking to the experience, but since this is too slow for survival purposes the amygdala will decide if there really is danger to your survival or whether you were just shocked by something that won't pose a threat, e.g. little Johnny jumping out at you from behind a door.

The amygdala also uses the experience data to produce your emotional response to the experience. If there is not an immediate threat the information is passed on for further processing to your logical brain but if there is danger the amygdala will produce fear which starts a behavioural chain reaction designed to protect you – your fight or flight reaction is triggered.

So what does this have to do with trading? Well, in our modern world the traditional dangers of wild animals and other predators have been replaced by less obvious threats – such as the threat to your money posed by a losing trade. These are perceived threats and can and do trigger a similar emotional and behavioural survival chain reaction that the presence of a sabre-toothed tiger might.

If the perceived threat is strong enough, i.e. we sense we will lose something important to us, the thalamus can and does bypass the sensory cortex and delivers the experience data direct to the fear-creating amygdala, resulting in knee-jerk reactions and incomprehensible actions like closing a trade too soon due to that fear.

Key point

Your emotions are important in trading and exist to tell you something important – so pay attention to what they are saying! Usually they are telling you to beware and think about what is happening to you.

The Trading Emotional Roller Coaster

Now we know something of how the brain functions and how this creates the emotions we experience, we can move on to examine some of the more common of these trading emotions and how they manifest in the trading experience.

Common trading emotions

In the table below we see some of the commonest emotions I have encountered when coaching my trader clients. This is a very short selection from the gamut of emotions we are able to experience at any moment. Although I have separated them into negative and positive emotions, that doesn't mean the emotion produced a desirable behaviour. Behaviours are discussed later in this article.

Negative Emotions	Positive Emotions
Fear of losing	Eagerness
Panic	Joy/Happiness
Disappointment	Euphoria
Impatience	Anticipation
Boredom	Excitement

How these emotions impact trading

It may be assumed that if you are experiencing a positive emotion, such as excitement, that this would naturally produce a positive and useful behaviour, but that may not be the case. In fact, what are perceived to be positive emotions may just as easily result in disastrous trading behaviours as the negative ones.

The reality is that any emotion can produce any type of behaviour, especially if the emotion is very strong. This is because the stronger the emotion the less able you are to utilise your frontal lobes because they become less active in the presence of strong emotions.

An example of this phenomenon is when someone is angry; normally an intense emotion. When anger is experienced it can be very difficult to not react with physical and often violent behaviour.

Key point

Strong emotions usually produce impulsive, and illogical, behaviours. For example, after losing a trade and feeling disappointed, you may feel compelled to enter a trade quickly in the hope of a quick win to try to feel better.

For most people, if you are experiencing a strong and intense emotion then you are not in the best condition for trading.

Identifying and controlling emotions

It is a powerful skill to be able to accurately identify the emotion you are experiencing in any given moment and circumstance. It is also a skill you can learn and develop so that you can tune in to yourself whenever you want to. This has two very important benefits: it gives you time to press the pause button on the processes at work within you, and this pause gives your logical brain a chance to activate and influence the behaviour resulting from the emotion.

In other words, you get time to stop and think and then decide on the best course of action to take in the immediate circumstances rather than allowing your emotion to dictate the way you act. This gives you options, which gives you control over yourself.

Which emotions are in play?

At any given moment you may be feeling more than one emotion, hence the expression "I have mixed emotions about ...". However, it is not possible to be experiencing two opposite emotions at the same moment. For example, you cannot be happy *and* sad at the same time. They can be experienced one at a time but never together. With similar emotions, you may be feeling more than one because the thoughts and chemical soup may be very similar for each. This may lead to confusion as to which emotions are in play.

To find out which emotion or emotions are at work prepare a mental list of the emotions you experience the most in your life and then tune in to your immediate feelings to find which emotion seems most appropriate for how you are feeling. Occasionally, with a brand-new experience may come an emotion you haven't experienced before hence the expression "I've never felt this way before ...".

Putting mixed emotions in order

If you identify more than one emotion at work then you can prioritise the various emotions simply using a dominance scale from 0 to 10. To do this, become aware of the dominant emotion in the moment and rate the intensity of that emotion from 0 to

10 (with 10 being the most intense feeling and 0 being no feeling). Then repeat this for whichever other emotions you are aware of.

The point of this exercise is that it is the most dominant emotions that will affect your choice of behaviour the most. Knowing which emotion is dominant and understanding your own behaviours (see later in this article) allows you to anticipate, and then change if necessary, what is likely to happen next, i.e. what action you are likely to take.

A simple technique to change any emotion

Since your emotions change very rapidly, and since they are strongly influenced by your thoughts and judgements about an experience, it is possible to change your emotion at will.

The quickest and easiest way to do this is utilising your storehouse of memories. Memories are formed from the data extracted from an experience combined with your emotional response to that experience. With this in mind, if you recall an experience with an emotion you desire, your entire psychological and physiological state will change as that memory is relived.

For example, if you feel angry simply recall a memory (or series of memories) of times when you were very calm and relaxed. This will have the effect of changing your chemical soup and your thoughts producing a calmer state and reducing or removing the anger.

Trading behaviours

We have explored the world of emotions and how we can become more aware of our own emotions. We have also learned a simple but effective technique for changing, and hence controlling, our emotional state at will. Let's now turn our attention to the behaviours produced by our emotions.

What is behaviour?

Again, keeping to the KISS idea, behaviours manifest as the actions you take. This covers everything from sitting still in a chair to climbing a mountain. Taking no action is also a behaviour since your chosen behaviour manifests as inaction; in this case the action or behaviour is to take no action.

In your trading, as in life in general, everything you do is created by a behaviour influenced by some emotion (at some psychological level). The question is whether the behaviour you choose to act upon is useful to you and what you are trying to achieve or not.

Key point

You choose how to behave: nobody and nothing makes you do what you do.

What factors contribute to your behaviour?

In this article the focus is on how emotions affect your trading but there are also several other factors that contribute to your choice of behaviour in any given situation; not least in your trading.

Some of the other important influences on your behaviour are:

- Your **Core Values** – the fabric of who you are as a person.

- Your **Beliefs** – learned from the influences in your life and/or given to you by others.

- Your **Attitudes** – these are formed from your judgements about things.

Each of these operates at a different psychological level and they also act as filters that sift through the information that is contributing to your chosen behaviour. A detailed exploration of these filters is beyond the scope of this article.

Your existing behaviours – useful or not

It is a very powerful and useful exercise to analyse your current trading behaviours. How do you behave while you trade? Specifically:

- What do you feel and how do you behave when you win a trade?

- What do you feel and how do you behave when you lose a trade?

- What do you feel and how do you behave when a trade is moving towards your target?

- What do you feel and how do you behave when a trade is moving away from your target?

The answers to these questions will give you a clearer idea of your trading feelings and behaviours. In other words your trading experience.

I encourage you, no I dare you, to do this analysis on yourself. It may not be a comfortable realisation but ultimately it will prove to be one of the best things you can do to increase your potential for trading success.

The key things to be looking to do with this exercise are:

- Identify the behaviour – what are you doing, specifically?

- Identify the emotion behind the behaviour – what is creating this emotion?

- Identify the purpose of the behaviour – what are you thinking and why are you doing that specific behaviour?

- Assess the effectiveness of the behaviour – is it really helping you? How?

- Choose a more useful behaviour – if necessary change an existing behaviour for something more useful to your trading.

- Create a way of reminding yourself (a trigger) to do the new behaviour to create a habit.

Create time right now for this very important exercise. You won't regret it!

Final thoughts

In this article I have discussed how your emotions lead to your behaviours and how both of these influence your trading experience. As you have been reading I imagine your mind has been actively making connections between what you are reading and your own experiences. This can produce valuable insights for you to heighten your own self-awareness!

If you have also taken the opportunity to complete the exercises I have provided (if not go back and do them – you and your trading will benefit from them but only if you do them), you will probably have a much better understanding of not only yourself but also your entire trading experience.

This greater self-awareness is the first step towards making any kind of positive change to your trading behaviours and all my new clients undertake a self-awareness exercise to get to know themselves at a deeper than normal level and to prepare themselves for positive change. The bottom line is, if you don't know and understand yourself and how and why you do things, it makes it difficult to know what to change and how best to change.

About Les Meehan

Les Meehan is an experienced soft-skills trainer and coach specialising in Success Behaviours to enhance performance and achievement using a variety of deep-mind techniques.

He engages internationally with traders to deliver performance-enhancing individual deep-mind coaching. Les also trains business directors and their teams in deep-mind influencing skills to create more effective leadership communication and produce more successful global business negotiators.

Les has a passion for working with traders who want to achieve their dreams. His focus is on finding and resolving any emotional drivers that will be negatively impacting on your trading performance and your ability to achieve the success you desire.

Les Meehan can be contacted through his website **www. rightmindtrader.com**, or by email at **les.meehan@ rightmindtrader.com**. Les is happy to offer readers of this book a 10% discount on his new trading course. Please quote TWTT2 to obtain this discount.

APPENDIX 4: CLIENT TRADE

Much of the material in this book has been the result of talking with clients; I will end the book with a trade done by one such client.

Entry

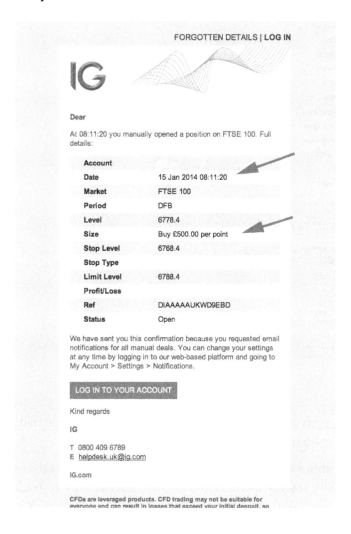

Exit

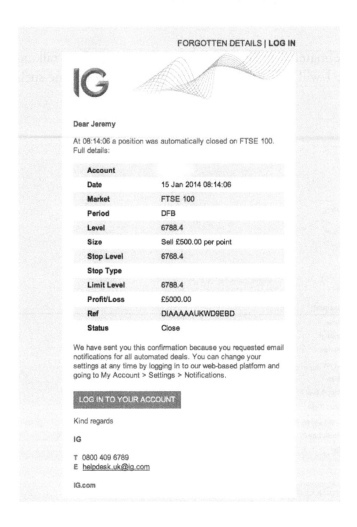

Those of you with a keen eye will have noticed that this single trade brought in £5000 in three minutes!

When I talk about the *business* of trading this is what I am talking about. So many traders spend hours at their screens only to trade in £5 or £10 per point – but no business can be run like that. You need to refine your technique and then go for it in sufficient size to make a difference.

Not everyone needs to trade at £500 per point but you do need to trade in size if you want to make real money in the markets.

I had originally placed this trade at the start of the book but my publisher felt this was a bit gimmicky. On reflection I agreed – a single trade in itself is not necessarily important. For example, it might be only one winner out of ten trades, or it may be a very small percentage of that particular trader's capital. In fact neither of those is the case here. To me, the trade shows what can be done and the ultimate simplicity of £5000 in three minutes sums up *trading as a business*!

APPENDIX 5: GUIDE TO JOHN PIPER SERVICES

As well as his numerous books, John offers a number of free and subscription services.

Free

For John's free service please go to **www.johnpiper.info/jptt.htm** (you will also receive a free copy of *Wealth is a Choice* and you will usually get two free reports each month).

Other

John runs the Big Call service, looking for the bigger moves in key markets, sells systems (such as *ZeitGap*), gives regular seminars, and is also happy to discuss professional trading if you want to make this your career.

(If ordering please quote the reference TWTT2BC as you will receive a discount and/or a bonus as you have read this book.)

For details on *ZeitGap* go to **www.zeitgap.com**

For details of the PROTRADER mentorship package go to **www.johnpiper.info/PROTRADER.htm**

Contact

You can contact John on **john@bigcall.co.uk**

Website – **www.johnpiper.info**

Support

For links, additional articles and videos please visit **twtt.johnpipersupport.com** and enter the password BOOK26.

THANKS

FOR READING!

Our readers mean everything to us at Harriman House. As a special thank you for buying this book, let us help you save as much as possible on your next read:

1

If you've never ordered from us before, get £5 off your first order at **harriman-house.com** with this code: wttb51

Already a customer? Get £5 off an order of £25 or more with this code: wttb25

2

Get 7 days' FREE access to hundreds of our books at **volow.co** – simply head to the website and sign up.

Thanks again!
from the team at

 Harriman House

Codes can only be used once per customer and order. T&Cs apply.